LOOK LIKE JESUS:
A GUIDE TO SPIRITUAL GROWTH

DR. ROGER L. BARRIER, JR.
BRIANNA BARRIER WETHERBEE

Copyright

DEDICATION

To Jessica Lynn, our little girl in heaven, who inspired this book.

ACKNOWLEDGMENTS

No one grows up alone. I remember getting up early and seeing my father down on his knees in prayer. He was praying for me, and our family and for a host of other things. Every child should be so blessed.

Thirteen of my formative years were spent under the pastoral care of W.W. Baker. He loved the Lord, and he loved people.

From Bill Weber, I learned I would be further along spiritually if I spent most of my ministry growing to be a spiritual man instead of trying to grow a large church through "big days" and promotions.

Albert Fox inculcated into me a love for physics and science. He was in the hospital with a brain tumor when he whispered quietly to me, "Watch closely. I want you to see how a Christian is supposed to die."

I remember the day my wife, Julie, left her prayer list open on the bed. I peeked at the seven things she was praying for me. The first was, "God, deliver Roger from the 'fear of man which brings a snare.' Make him more concerned with what You think than with what the people think."

Many pastors and writers whom I've never met are my mentors. I read their books. *Principles of Spiritual Growth*[1] by Miles Stanford is a short collection of letters describing basic spiritual growth principles. Each chapter can be summarized in one short sentence. Try it. You'll like it.

Watchman Nee has two books that will spur us on toward spiritual maturity. *The Release of the Spirit*[2] demonstrates how God processes us so people can see Jesus living within us. His three-volume, *The Spiritual Man*[3] describes the workings of our spirit, soul, and body to further our development as spiritual mothers and fathers. This is a long work. If all you read is volume one that's probably enough.

Hannah Hurnard's, *Hinds' Feet on High Places*[4]. "Hind" is a British word for a female deer. The book is an allegory describing spiritual growth along the lines of John Bunyan's *Pilgrim's Progress*[5]. *Hinds' Feet* is a careful rendering of the processing God uses to bring spiritual children to full spiritual maturity. The goal of maturity is not to sit on the High Places enjoying unlimited delight in the presence of God. Maturity means returning to the Valley of Humiliation and giving away our lives to bring in the Kingdom of God on earth.

Her return to the valley is documented in her sequel, *Mountains of Spices*[6]. As I finished the sequel, sitting in an airplane at the end of a runway waiting to take off, I had to explain to the stranger next to me why I was weeping.

Jeanne Guyon was a fourteenth-century French woman who wrote the Christian classic, *Experiencing the Depths of Jesus Christ*[7]. Her belief that anyone, anywhere, anytime can enter directly into fellowship with Christ conflicted with the prevailing Roman Catholic teaching that Christ can only be approached through a Catholic priest. Her book comes to us through the looking glass of persecution. Respect it as such. This is a most tender and practical book on how to enter into intimacy with God.

Finally, I am indebted to David Ferguson for developing a biblical theology of relationships. Read more about relationship theology in *Intimate Encounters*[8] and *Relational Foundations*[9].

Scores of other mentors, leaders, friends, associates, and family members have helped to shape my insights into the spiritual life. May they all be blessed. Thanks to all of you.

CONTENTS

INTRODUCTION

The Baby Who Couldn't Grow Up

Our firstborn child died in our arms. We were having dinner when Julie said, "Roger, she's gone."

Jessie's DNA was abnormal. She had three chromosomes instead of the customary two in the 18th pair. Trisomy 21 produces Down syndrome. Jessie had Trisomy 18. Trisomy 18 produces a mishmash of confused genetic instructions. Her poorly formed heart wasn't strong enough to support her tiny body. We knew she was destined soon to die.

Occasionally, I've heard people say, "Oh, isn't that a cute little baby? Wouldn't it be nice if she could always stay that size?"

No. No! It is not nice. It is not a good thing. I had a little baby who couldn't grow up; it was awful.

We were in the hospital for 40 days. I remember complaining to God, "How come that woman gets a healthy baby? She gets to take hers home. This is not fair! Why did we get the baby who is going to die?"

The most difficult prayer Julie and I ever prayed was on a Sunday evening about eight months after we left the hospital. Totally exhausted from full-time pastoring and around the clock childcare, Julie and I asked God to go ahead and let Jessie die. Six days later, she was in heaven.

We were in the hospital for exactly 40 days.

What Would Never Be

Jessie cost us everything we had. Hospital costs and weekly doctor visits continued long after she was released from the hospital. After nine agonizing months, she died. The expenses finally stopped.

If she were still here, she would be all grown-up now. I hurt when I think of all the great times we missed together. I have delightful memories with my other daughters. I don't have any memories like that with Jessie. I would have enjoyed Jessie's high school graduation, but she didn't have one. I would give anything to have seen the excited smile on her face as I walked her down the aisle at her wedding. I remember that moment with my other daughters, Brianna and Bronwyn. But Jessie and I never experienced that together. What I wouldn't give to have watched her hold her firstborn child! But that never happened.

Occasionally, I still pull off to the side of the road and weep at what was never to be.

Grief and Questions

As the initial shock of her death wore off, I began to realize I was intensely angry with God: "Is this the way You treat Your children? Julie and I have dedicated our lives to You! We poured our lives into Your service. We dedicated our family to You. Is this the thanks we get?"

In James 1:5, God invites us to ask for His insight when we struggle to understand why He allows trials in our lives. I was praying one morning, and I asked Him, "What are you doing with Julie and me?" Deep down in my innermost spirit, I heard God speak: "Roger, do you know how much it hurts you to have a little baby who can't grow up physically?"

"Yes, God. It really hurts."

"Roger, I gave you Jessie so you might have a tiny taste of how I feel when one of my newborn-again children fails to grow up."

I am convinced the greatest tragedy in the Christian church is the believer who fails to grow up.

LEVELS OF SPIRITUAL MATURITY

"Every man is just as spiritual as he wants to be."

Before we go another step further, I must ask if you read the *Introduction* and *Acknowledgement*? Most people want to jump right in with chapter one. However, it is important that you read both. So, if you skipped over them, please go back and read them, and then you may move on to chapter one.

In John 21:15-18, Jesus was restoring Peter after denying Jesus three times! Jesus told his disciples to meet with him in Jerusalem. But they disobeyed and returned to the Sea of Galilee and reopened their fishing business. After fishing all night, and catching nothing, they heard a voice yelling for them to cast their nets on the other side of the boat. When they did, they caught more fish than the boat could hold. Suddenly, Peter recognized the Lord and jumped out of the boat and swam to the shore where Jesus was cooking breakfast.

After breakfast Jesus said to Peter, "Do you love me more than these? Peter said, "Yes Lord, you know that I love you." Jesus said, "Feed my lambs."

It's important to know that Jesus was making a distinction here. The word for "love" that Jesus used was "agape." Agape love is divine love which never stops. Agape love loves the unlovable.

But the word Peter used in return was "philos." This word means "friend" or "brother." How could Peter say that he loved Jesus with agape love when he had denied Jesus three times and then returned to his fishing business? "Philos" was the best he could do. Jesus then said, "Feed my lambs."

Again, Jesus said, "Simon son of John, do you "agape" me?" He answered, "Yes Lord, you know that I "philos" you. Jesus said, "Take care of my sheep."

The third time Jesus said to him, "Simon, son of John, do you even "philos" me? Peter was hurt because Jesus asked him for the third time. So Peter said, "Lord, you know all things; you know that I philos you." Jesus said, "Feed my sheep."

Jesus is giving Peter a new job description. Early in Jesus' ministry he called Peter to fish for men. He was an evangelist. Now Jesus was commissioning Peter to do the things that a shepherd does. He is to shepherd the flock of Christ on earth. Jesus said, "Feed my lambs" and "Take care of my sheep."

Notice that Jesus recognized at least two levels of spiritual growth. Some are lambs and some are sheep.

In 1 Corinthians 1:3 Paul, describes another level: Babies!

Brothers, I could not address you as spiritual, but as worldly mere infants in Christ. I gave you milk, not solid food for you were not yet ready for it. Indeed, you are still not ready. You are worldly. For since there is jealousy and quarreling among you, are you not worldly are you not acting like mere men?

The Greek word we translate in English as "worldly" has two different nuances. First, it describes spiritual infants with soft baby-like flesh. Second, it describes Christians who started out as babies, but soon became hardened like a piece of gristle-filled meat ... tough and hard to chew.

The Christians in Corinth started out under Paul's leadership as spiritual babies. The tragedy was that after three years, they were still babies. Mark it, if you're still a baby Christian after three years, then you're on the way to becoming hardened to spiritual things.

Peter pleaded with his hearers to grow up. As infants, they could handle only milk. He encouraged them to grow up so they could chew on the deeper things of God (see 1 Peter 2:2).

In 1 John 2:12-14, the apostle John describes at least three levels of maturity:

> *I write to you, dear children, because your sins have been forgiven on account of his name. I write to you, fathers, because you have known him who is from the beginning.*
>
> *I write to you, young men, because you have overcome the evil one. I write to you, dear children, because you have known the Father.*
>
> *I write to you, fathers, because you have known him who is from the beginning.*
>
> *I write to you, young men, because you are strong, and the word of God lives in you, and you have overcome the evil one.*

Notice that John listed two distinct characteristics of spiritual children. Their sins are forgiven, and they have known God the father. He declares three distinct characteristics of spiritual young men and women. They know the Word of God, they are strong, and they have overcome the evil one. He describes only one distinctive characteristic of spiritual mothers and fathers ... but he repeats it twice.

We will describe numerous characteristics of children, young men women, and mothers and fathers in upcoming chapters.

Whenever I teach my spiritual growth class, I began by asking the folks to think about their spiritual level.

I ask them to raise their hands.

How many of you think that you are a spiritual child? About 30% of the hands go up.

How many of you think that you are a spiritual man or woman? About 20% of the hands go up.

How many of you consider yourself to be spiritual mothers or fathers? Fully 50% raise their hands.

Several months later, after we work through the Bible's principles of spiritual growth, I ask the same question.

How many of you consider yourself to be spiritual children? At least 50% of the hands go up.

Only four or five consider themselves to be a spiritual mother or father. I've discovered that most of us will tend to think that we are further along on the journey than we really are. We have much to learn and to experience.

Baby Christians who choose to remain babies do so for many reasons. Some reject the gospel and drop out before they begin. Some drop out early because they can't handle the persecution that comes with following Christ. Some drop out because earthly distractions are so alluring. They trade the eternal for the temporary.

Some are so arrogant that they rarely seek the Father's guidance. Some babies imagine that whatever they don't already know is not really necessary. How tragic!

Some babies aren't lazy at work or at home or with their hobbies; but they are lazy and inattentive to spiritual things. The Bible is to be studied diligently. The spiritual life is to be cultivated and lived with endurance and consistency. God will not force-feed His children. He waits until they are hungry; then He feeds them.

Christians who neglect to grow up are in danger of becoming hardened and insensitive to the promptings of God—or even worse—of slipping and sliding back away from Christ.

Let me give you an example of what happened to one who didn't make it.

Demas was a close friend and companion of the apostle Paul. Unfortunately, Demas failed to grow, and ultimately slid away from Christ.

Notice his downward regression into apostasy.

Our first picture of him is as a fellow worker of Christ. He was on fire for Jesus.

"And so do Mark, Aristarchus, Demas and Luke, my fellow workers" Philemon 1:24 (NIV).

The next time we see him he is just Demas. There is no praising appellation. Something is happening and he is not burning quite as brightly.

"Our dear friend Luke, the doctor, and Demas send greetings" Colossians 4:14 (NIV).

Finally, unfortunately, he took his eyes off Jesus and was attracted on the world.

> *"For Demas, because he loved this world, has deserted me and has gone to Thessalonica" (2 Timothy 4:10 NIV).*

Three brief mentions show the apostasy of a man who started fast with Jesus and didn't make it to the end.

In the latter days of her life, my mother refused to use her walker. We were not at all surprised when she fell and broke her hip. She was in agony. Shortly after surgery, she was forced to get up and walk in order to rebuild her rapidly deteriorating muscles. The alternative was never to get out of bed again.

During the first session with the physical therapist, my mom yelled again and again, "Stop it! Stop it! You're hurting me!" The young woman patiently explained that she had done this many times and knew what was best.

My mom replied, "You do not know best. I know better than you do what I need!" She refused to get out of bed because it hurt.

Later that night, I was exercising Mom's leg. She was not happy. She wanted to be left alone. No matter how I moved it, she hurt; she cried out in pain; she begged me to stop.

I patiently explained how I loved her too much to stop—even if it did hurt. She looked at me with anger and said slowly and deliberately: "And I thought you were the good son."

Mom chose not to tolerate the pain of physical therapy—and walked with a painful, shuffling gait for the rest of her life.

She reminds me of baby Christians who refuse to grow up.

The progression from spiritual childhood to young man/womanhood to father/motherhood parallels the spiritual progression of the three periods of Moses' 120-year life. Moses spent the first part of his life thinking he was somebody important. He was a prince of Egypt, raised in the palace by Pharaoh's daughter. Tradition tells us that he was a powerful soldier who led a successful military campaign against the Ethiopians during a border dispute in southern Egypt. Moses spent his first forty years in Egypt full of self-reliance.

When he was forty, he began sensing the pain and suffering of his Hebrews brothers and sisters. He murdered an Egyptian who was whipping a Hebrew slave. Fearing capture and punishment, he fled Egypt.

From age forty to eighty, Moses tended sheep in the deserts of Midian. He was a "nobody"—useless to God and man. He suffered debilitating bouts of self-condemnation during this second third of his life, as evidenced by his response when God called him to lead His people out of Egypt. Kneeling beside the burning bush at the age of eighty, he confessed, "God, I can't do it. Surely, you don't want me! Why don't you use my brother, Aaron?" (See Exodus 3-4). God, I don't even know your name!"

But God had plans for Moses. He spent the last forty years of his life discovering what God can do with anybody. With the rod of God, Moses confronted Pharaoh, instigated disastrous plagues, split the Red Sea, and led the Hebrew slaves out of Egypt and up to the threshold of the Promised Land.

God loves to take nobodies and turn them into somebodies. He demonstrated with Moses what He can do with anybody!

The growth process John outlined implies a long-term commitment. Nothing less than wholehearted devotion will suffice. The process is not for the faint of heart. However, along the way, we will increasingly experience the deepening love and resurrection power of Christ. We can't help but develop an irresistible urge to become like Christ at any price.

In *Principles of Spiritual Growth,* Miles Stanford laid out the process God employs in molding us to maturity:

> *It is more than comforting to realize that it is those who have plumbed the depths of their own failure to whom God invariably gives the call to shepherd others. ...*
>
> *It takes a man who has discovered something of his own weakness to be patient with the foibles of others. ... The Lord does not give the charge, "Shepherd my sheep" ... on hearing Peter's self-confident affirmation of undying loyalty. He gives it after Peter has failed to keep his vows and has wept bitterly in the streets of Jerusalem.[12]*

Reflect on what you've just read. Think of your own spiritual level. How far along have you come?

Now, not too quickly, with thought, meaning and surrender, let's pray our prayer:

> *Dear Father,*
>
> *Thank you for the progress I've made together with you in my spiritual journey. Please nurture me along the path of maturity at any price.*
>
> *Amen.*

CHAPTER TWO

THE HIKING TRAIL

God intends to shepherd His children from the valleys below to the mountain tops of spiritual maturity.

The hiking path was covered with melting snow. The Swiss Alps were breathtaking, stretching out in a 360° panorama of visual delight. My wife, Julie, daughter Bronwyn and I looked up at the Eiger train station about 500 feet above us.

"Do you want to go a little further or head back down?" I asked. The station looked so close. We decided to keep going.

We soon came to a fork in the trail. Far in the distance we saw a hiker waving his arms towards us. But he was too far away to see him well or hear him yell.

We picked the pass on our right and continued our ascent. Too late, I realized that we'd chosen the wrong path. We were now above the tree line. The trail was so steep that we could barely climb. The mountains looming above were loaded with snow. I couldn't see the station anymore. It was several hundred feet below. We were on the wrong ridge.

Julie collapsed on the trail and began to weep: "I can't go any farther."

"Yes, you can," I said, "We can't stop now!"

I panicked. The snow field between us and the train station on the other ridge looked absolutely impassable. I was paralyzed with fear.

Bronwyn was a snowboarder with some measure of experience in snow fields. "Stop it! Stop it, Dad!" she shouted at me. "If you panic, we'll all be lost. Get hold of yourself."

I forced my emotions back under control.

"I'll lead the way across the snow to the other ridge," she said. "You and Mom step exactly in my footsteps."

I literally said, "I now place the leadership of our family in your hands. I am abdicating control to you." Forty-five minutes later, we reached the safety of the station.

We were eating lunch when a German hiker approached our table. He was angry. "Why didn't you listen to me? You were up in the avalanche zone. You were stupid. Before you try a stunt like that again, get a guide who knows what he's doing."

By the way, when we finished lunch, I took back control of the family.

In this chapter we will overview the pathway that Jesus has laid out for us from infancy to full-blown spiritual mothers and fathers. God the Father challenges us to complete the journey at any price.

Taking Our First Steps

Notice how many people are milling around outside the door of salvation. According to Jesus they are lost in their sins and without a Savior.

There's not enough room to go through the door burdened with a backpack of our selfish will and a miasma of sins. When we receive Christ as our Lord and Savior our backpack is emptied of sin. Now there is just enough room to squeeze through the door. As we crawl through the tiny door, we are "born again" into the family of God (see John 3:3-8).

> *Enter through the narrow gate. For wide is the gate and broad is the road that leads to destruction, and many enter through it. But small is the gate and narrow the road that leads to life, and only a few find it"* (Matthew 7:13-14 NIV).

Notice how the line grows upward. This represents our growth from infants, to children, to spiritual young men and women, and on to mothers and fathers.

As we move through childhood, we begin to discover that the cross of Christ has two functions.

First, Jesus died on the cross for me. The cross of salvation provides for our salvation from the dastardly effects of sin and wickedness. God placed Christ on the cross of salvation in order to deliver us from the domination of our sin nature (see Galatians 3:13). Romans 6:23 teaches, "The wages of sin is death; but the gift of God is eternal life through Jesus Christ our Lord" (NIV).

Second, I died with Jesus on the cross of sanctification. God uses the cross of sanctification to mold us to look like Jesus; "I have been crucified with Christ and I no longer live, but Christ lives in me" (Galatians 2:20 NIV).

Receiving Christ as our personal Savior makes us fit for heaven. God working through the cross of sanctification makes us fit to live on earth.

Sanctification is the process by which God molds us on earth to be what He already sees us to be in Heaven.

CROSS OF SANCTIFICATION

DOOR OF SALVATION

LOST   INFANT CHILDREN   YOUNG MEN & WOMEN   MOTHERS & FATHERS

The cross of sanctification in the middle of the chasm on the chart represents the struggles, trials, difficulties, and sufferings which God uses to mature us to look like Jesus. The cross of sanctification often results in a myriad of pains. However, keep in mind that the cross is not an end in itself.

Remember, no one ever had a resurrection without first experiencing a cross.

Spiritual children struggle with accepting some of the difficulties they face. "Dear God, if you really loved me you would never let this happen to me!" They often get angry when things don't go the way that they want, because they have yet to recognize God's hand at work.

Notice on the chart that spiritual mothers and fathers are walking on the mountaintops of spiritual maturity. Intimacy with Jesus is increasing. By the way, one of the major responsibilities of spiritual mothers and fathers is to descend from the heights and invest their lives in caring for those not quite as far along the journey as they.

As we move through childhood, we stand at the edge of a precipice. The cross of sanctification stands in the middle of the journey. Will we go on with Christ or not? Will we go on to maturity and one day reach the spiritual mountain peaks beyond? Or, will we backtrack to the door of salvation because the cost is too high.

We have to ask ourselves; "Am I willing to follow Christ at any price?"

Not long after our spiritual birth, God shows us that we didn't surrender as much of ourselves as we imagined. We still cling to our fallen nature, our sins, and our old ways. "My way vs. God's way" is a constant struggle—especially for babies and children.

Look at the traffic jam of worldly, hardened children huddled back at the door of salvation. On the other hand, there are a few who hate the chains that bind so deeply, that they surrender to God's work on the cross at any price.

Over more than fifty years of ministry, my impression is that fewer than ten percent choose to go on. Over ninety percent turn back. The cost is too high for them. By grace, they are still inside the door of salvation—but just barely.

> By the grace God has given me, I laid a foundation as an expert builder, and someone else is building on it. But each one should be careful how he builds. For no one can lay any foundation other than the one already laid, which is Jesus Christ.
>
> If any man builds on this foundation using gold, silver, costly stones, wood, hay or straw, his work will be shown for what it is, because the day will bring it to light. It will be revealed with fire, and the fire will test the quality of each man's work.
>
> If what is built survives, he will receive his reward. If it is burned up, he will suffer loss; he himself will be saved, but only as one escaping through the flames." (1 Corinthians 3:10-15 NIV)

Crossing the Chasm

When I was a boy, I put on my Halloween costume and longed for the neighbors to fill my trick-or-treat bag with the "good stuff"—chocolate bars, Snickers, Baby Ruths, Almond Joys, Milky Ways and so forth. Lollipops and bubble gum were "bad stuff." Think of the cross of sanctification as a tool for cleaning out the gum and lollipops and leaving the "good stuff" behind.

By the way, no one can make an end run from childhood to mother or fatherhood without going through the cross of sanctification.

People fall away from Jesus for numerous reasons. Some of the most damaging are pride, laziness, worldly distractions, sexual involvement; deceit; hypocrites, disappointment in God or God's people, persecution, betrayal ,and a rampantly sinful culture—just to name a few.

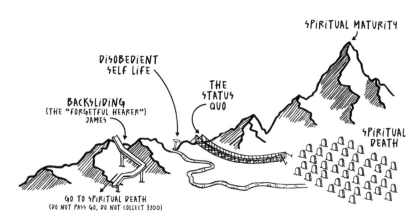

Don't think for a moment that those Christians who decide not to face crucifixion on the cross of sanctification are safe from God's processing. God has no intention of leaving them alone. He will do whatever it takes to get them back on the road to maturity. Even when it hurts.

It's best to surrender wholeheartedly to Christ today ... or face the music later on. I love the saying, "Respond well to God's little taps and thus avoid his mighty raps."

> *Our fathers disciplined us for a little while as they thought best; but God disciplines us for our own good that we may share in his holiness. No discipline seems pleasant at the time, but painful, later on however, it produces a harvest of righteousness and peace for those who have been trained by it.* (Hebrews 12:10-11 NIV)

Notice that those who say, "No," don't stay at the same spiritual level as when they backed off. They don't maintain the status quo. They slide back downward into disobedient self-life and become what James calls "forgetful hearers" (see James 1:22-24).

Jesus described these people as those who have lost their first love for Him.

I've counseled many people who regret slipping away from Christ and who now want to return to godly living and a deepening, intimate relationship with Christ.

In writing to the church at Ephesus Jesus gives a three-point program of how to return if you've lost your first love (see Revelation 2:1-8):

1. Remember what it was like when you first fell in love with Jesus.

2. Repent that it's not that way.

3. Repeat the things you used to do when you first fell in love with Jesus.

Choosing to follow Jesus is an ongoing, daily struggle. Many of my students try to figure out what is the one big cross experience that they will face. But, as you see in the diagram above, there is not just one big cross in one big chasm. There are many little crosses in many little chasms. Jesus explained this in Luke 9:23:

> If anyone would come after me, he must deny himself and take up his cross daily and follow me. (NIV)

The journey to the high places is a daily activity.

Christians who choose not to go on are stymied. Their growth is imperiled in a disobedient-self life as they reach that same dead end.

Unfortunately, God does not hold our spiritual place in line until we decide to return to the upward journey. Once we stop, we initiate a process identified in the book of Jeremiah as "backsliding" (see 2:19; 3:22; 14:7; and 15:6).

They are in a process that I call "spiritual retrograde." During our stymied period, we do not hold our ground. We do not maintain the status quo. We actually "forget" things that we knew and slide back to an earlier stage of growth. As long as we choose not to grow up, we will continue spiritual retrogression.

The practice of asking for a person's "John Hancock" traces back to the ostentatious signature on the American Declaration of Independence by John Hancock. His name stands out ten times larger than any other's name. He deliberately scrawled his name in large, flowing letters, to be certain that King George III of England could read his name without the aid of glasses. It was a bold declaration of his personal commitment to do whatever was necessary to defeat England's hold over the new American colonies.

He was considered by England to be a traitor. King George offered amnesty to all Americans who were willing to lay down their arms. Hancock was singled out by King George III as one who would never receive amnesty!

Every Christian is to sign our "John Hancock" to the Lord Jesus Christ.

The levels of spiritual maturity are fluid. The further along we are in our journeys, the more time we spend on the resurrection side of the cross. At times, spiritual children will experience some of the heights, but they don't stay there long.

About ten years after I entered the ministry, I needed some personal counseling. During the third session, my counselor and I were discussing an issue from my past when he said, "You know, Roger, most people settle this issue when they are thirteen years old."

"Did you just call me immature?"

"Well, in this particular area, yes."

I was in my 30s, but I still had troubling issues related to my adolescence.

Just because we are growing spiritually does not mean that we've conquered or surpassed all the issues of childhood or adolescence. Spiritual mothers and fathers can struggle at times with fear, commitment, and/or dependence just like spiritual children and young men and women. But in general, as we move through the stages of maturity, we leave those younger issues farther behind.

Thank God that we don't have to wait until we are spiritual mothers or fathers to enjoy the blessings of the resurrected life! Anytime, anywhere, anybody on any spiritual level can yield in obedience to the promptings and leadings of the Holy Spirit and enjoy moments of deep spirituality. However, we soon turned back to childhood. The same holds true for spiritual young men and women.

Paul laid out the foundations for Christian maturity in Philippians 3:10:

I want to know Christ, and the power of his resurrection and the fellowship of his sufferings. (NIV)

Keying off Philippians 3:10, I often ask my classes, "How many of you want to know deep intimacy with Christ?" Every hand goes up.

"How many of you want to know the resurrection power of Jesus Christ?" Every hand goes up.

"How many of you want to experience the fellowship of sharing in His sufferings?" Not one hand goes up. Then, after a moment of reflection, sometimes one hand or another will tentatively raise . . . but not often.

We all want to know Christ. We all want to experience the power of his resurrection. But we're not so interested in welcoming the cross of sanctification.

In our own sufferings, we have a personal link to Christ's own sufferings. Job declared, *"But he knows the way that I take; when he has tested me, I will come forth as gold"* (23:10 NIV).

A pastor friend of mine was having congregational troubles. He was in the process of losing his church, his house, and maybe even his marriage. In deep despair, he was contemplating whether or not to tender his resignation and leave the ministry.

One of his elders said, "You need to get some rest and a fresh perspective before you make some foolish decisions. I am scheduled to take a trip to the Holy Land, and I want you to go in my place. I'll cover all your expenses."

Several weeks later, my friend was walking through the Garden of Gethsemane thinking about his struggles. His mind gravitated to the sufferings Christ experienced in that very place. He decided to enter into the fellowship of Christ's sufferings. He shared,

I made my way to the small anteroom adjoining the church in the Garden. I got on my knees and began to pray. Everyone else was on the bus and ready to leave.

As I knelt, God began to overwhelm me with a small measure of the torment Christ experienced that night in the Garden. I remember sobbing uncontrollably.

The door opened and the tour director entered the room. He was looking for me. I was holding up the tour bus. I opened my eyes and saw blood coving the front of my shirt, pouring from my nose and dripping all over the floor. The director took out his handkerchief and we cleaned me up as best we could.

My pastor friend reached in his pocket, pulled out a blood-stained handkerchief, and said, "I carry this with me as a reminder of Gethsemane. I have a softer heart for Jesus as He grieves over the pain and suffering of our world".

As we grow spiritually, the cross is not viewed as a threat to our wellbeing; it is, instead, the instrument that makes possible the resurrection life of Christ.

We'll talk more about this later, but it's theologically correct to experience the feelings that Jesus feels when He sees the suffering and pain in our world—and then to comfort Him.

In the garden, Jesus asked the disciples to pray for Him as he struggled with the impending doom of the cross. The pain was so intense that He sweated blood mixed with tears.

The disciples were sound asleep when he returned. Listen to the disappointment in His words, "Could you not pray for me one hour. I only asked for an hour."

He wanted their comfort, but they failed. So, God sent some angels to do what He wanted the disciples to do. They comforted Him.

It's okay for us to weep with Jesus when He weeps. It's not good to weep alone. This is one dimension of entering into the fellowship of His sufferings.

Trusting Our Guide

Often as we walk the pathway to maturity, God engineers various experiences test our faith and commitment.

We must be careful here. We may never again face a more intense spiritual moment. We stand perplexed. It looks, from all outward appearances, like He's misled us, mistreated us or deserted us. Our faith falters. Will I still follow Him? Will I completely surrender my life to His hands?

How we handle this moment—and others like it—may well be the defining moments of our spiritual journeys from one level to the next. God challenges our commitment. He tests our dependence. We experience the cross, and only then may we experience true resurrection.

As we think about the cross of sanctification that we must face, we might find ourselves frightened or discouraged. Do not despair. God will give us all the power and grace that we could ever need for the journey ahead.

YOU HAVE ALL THE SPIRITUAL EQUIPMENT YOU NEED FOR THE JOURNEY

He not only provides a detailed map for the journey; He guarantees that we're never alone. Not only are we travelling in the presence of Christ, we're traveling in the company of many others—just like us—who are choosing to follow Jesus at any price.

Dear Father,

Please make the hiking trail so clear that I can't miss it. Keep me on the right path. Place my feet in the footprints of those who precede me. Give me strength, endurance, and friends to accompany me on the journey. Mature me into a spiritual mother/father at any price.

Amen.

CHAPTER THREE

SPIRITUAL CHILDREN

Spiritual children know that their sins are forgiven and that God is their Father.
(1 John 2:12-14 NIV)

Early one morning at about 5:00 a.m. Julie and I were awakened by our six-year-old daughter, Brianna, screaming, "Bronwyn threw up in bed! "Bronwyn threw up in bed! I said to Julie, "I'll take the sheets, you take Bronwyn."

I was thinking, "All we need now is a bunch of 'throw-up' viruses in the house. Please, Lord, don't let Julie or me get the virus."

Suddenly, Bronwyn lifted her arms and cried, "Hug? Hug?"

"Oh, great," I thought, "now I'll get the virus for sure!" Nevertheless, I picked her up, held her close, and whispered, "Why don't we go to the blue chair, and I'll rock you back to sleep."

So, we did. By the way, I didn't get the virus.

Bronwyn covered with vomit it is not a pretty sight. Nevertheless, when she held up her hands and said "Hug? Hug?" I immediately swooped her up into in my arms.

Covered with our sin, we, too, are not a very attractive sight to Jesus. Nevertheless, we can raise our hands and cry softly, "Lord, help! Hug? Hug?" Out of His mercy and love, our Father picks us up and pours the saving grace of new life deep within our souls.

In the next several chapters, we will interact with the characteristics of spiritual children, young men and women, and spiritual mothers and fathers. My hope is that you will develop a good sense of how far along you are on your spiritual journey, learn how to reach spiritual maturity, and discover a deep passion to grow to look like Jesus at any price.

Now we turn to chapter three and examine some characteristics of spiritual children.

Sins Forgiven

Spiritual children are forgiven of their sins because of Jesus' work on the cross:

> *"This is my blood which is shed for you."* (Matthew 26:28 NIV)

I had open-heart surgery when I was 13. The doctors diagnosed a hole in my heart.

The hospital blood bank was running drastically low on blood supply, so, they called for volunteers to come to the hospital and give blood for surgery patients. Dick Dickens, one of my childhood mentors, answered the call. He gave several pints of his blood for me. I'll never look at him the same way again.

By the way, the doctors made a mistake; "We're sorry, we opened your heart looking for the hole and there was none. So, we sewed you back up. You have a perfect heart."

But the scar tissue damaged my heart permanently. I've lived with the consequences of their mistake ever since.

The Apostle Paul declared: "All have sinned and fallen short of the glory of God" (Romans 3:23 NIV). He told of the devastation of unforgiven sin:

> *For the wages of sin is death, but the gift of God is eternal life in Christ Jesus our Lord.* (Romans 6:23 NIV)

Jesus died on the cross in our place. By shedding his blood and surrendering his life on the cross, He paid the penalty for all our sin. Now, we no longer have to pay the price for our sin.

Next, no one is born a Christian. Following Christ is a personal decision of the will. The process of confession, repentance, and forgiveness allows Jesus to forgive our sins and make us fit for heaven.

Of course, He has yet to make us fit to live on earth. That comes with the cross of sanctification, which we will dig into with later.

Forgiveness of sin is a free gift, but it doesn't come automatically. The gift is received by accepting Christ personally:

> *Yet to all who received him, to those who believed in his name, he gave the right to become children of God.* (John 1:12 NIV)

I've been threatened with death on four different occasions. I own two bulletproof vests. Before one Sunday morning service, my SWAT team coordinator briefed me on how to respond if the shooter made his move while I was greeting guests.

Les said, "If he comes at you, your job is to jump behind me."

I thought he was kidding.

He looked me and said firmly, "If he presents himself, you jump behind me; I'll take the bullet for you."

By dying on the cross, Jesus took the bullet for us.

Father God

Spiritual children know that God is their spiritual father.

> *"I write to you, dear children, because you have known the Father"* (1 John 2:1)

If your dad tucked you into bed at night, read you stories, gave you his approval, prayed goodnight prayers, pulled up the covers, and kissed your forehead as he said, "See you in the morning," then it is easy to think of God as your Father.

Unfortunately, not everyone had a good dad. If you and your brothers and sisters you under the bed when dad came home high or drunk, then thinking of God as your father may do more to conjure up painful hurts and emotions than to bring thoughts of compassion and security.

My grandfather was not a very good guy. My mom and her sisters often hid under the bed when he came home drunk. He committed suicide when I was four-years old.

My mom overcame much of her dysfunctional upbringing. She and God had a great relationship. However, when she contracted thyroid cancer, she struggled to understand why God allowed her to endure such suffering. "If You loved me, You wouldn't let these things happen to me. Sometimes, I wonder if You're real?"

When troubles assault us, many spiritual children struggle with doubts about God's compassion and care. As we worked through her struggles, my mom began to realize that many of her current feelings were really issues that came from her father.

Is it any surprise that she found it hard to pray the words, "Our Father"?

People who grew up in dysfunctional families need special compassion and care from those further along the spiritual journey. Wounded children must be led to see the heart of the real God before they can ever embrace Him as Father.

The Boss

Spiritual children often struggle to understand that Jesus is the boss and they are not.

After twelve years of living on a noisy-busy street, Julie and I decided that we had enough. It was time to move.

As we drove toward our new house, our four-year-old daughter Bronwyn announced, "Dad, you were the boss of the old house. *I'm* going to be the boss of the new house."

We laughed. But she really meant it. You should have lived with her during her teenage years!

Hopefully, sooner or later, spiritual children must come to grips with the idea that Jesus is the boss. After all, that's why we call him Lord.

Dependent on Others

All spiritual children are dependent on others for their care and feeding. No one would think of placing a newborn baby in front of the refrigerator and saying, "Bread and turkey are in the refrigerator for when you get hungry. Help yourself. Slice as much meat as you want. Go easy on the mayonnaise. The peanut butter is next to the pickles. By the way, the toilet is down this hall, second door on the left. Make yourself at home."

Spiritual children are ill-equipped to mature on their own. They are just learning how to take care of themselves More mature Christians have an awesome responsibility to help the less mature grow up. Peter reminded the church leaders of Ephesus:

> *To the elders among you, I appeal as a fellow elder . . . Be shepherds of God's flock that is under your care, serving as overseers—not because you must, but because you are willing, as God wants you to be.* (1 Peter 5:1 NIV)

Applying the Scriptures

Spiritual children are learning how to apply the Scriptures in their everyday lives.

Of course, we must know the Bible before we can begin to apply God's Word to ourselves. We will talk more about knowing the Bible well as we discuss spiritual young men and women in the next chapter.

> *Anyone who lives on milk, being still an infant, is not acquainted with the teaching about righteousness. But solid food is for the mature, who by constant use have trained themselves to distinguish good from evil.* (Hebrews 5:13–14 NIV)

Handling the Bible properly involves far more than just learning its content. Handling it well implies the ability to apply God's Word with wisdom and discernment.

I was late for a seminary class when I really cut off the driver in front of me. I was really in a hurry. However, what I did to him was not only rude; it was dangerous.

We came to a red light and I decided to stop about 40 feet back so I would not have to face him. However, he stopped 40 feet behind the red light as well. As he was rolling down the window to give me a piece of his mind, I remembered:

> *A gentle answer turns away wrath, but a harsh word stirs up anger.* (Proverbs 15:1 NIV)

Before he could finish opening the window, I shouted, "I'm so sorry. What I did was mean and nasty and totally wrong. "Will you please forgive me?"

He was caught completely by surprise. He stumbled out the words, "Well, I guess it's all right. Just don't ever let it happen again."

Spiritual children must not only learn the Scriptures; they must apply them as they journey on to become spiritual mothers and fathers. Let me give you another example.

> Be sure you know the condition of your flocks, give careful attention to your herds; for riches do not endure forever, and the crown is not secure for all generations." (Proverbs 27:23 NIV)

What's the application for this passage?

Make yourself a budget. The only way to control money properly is to have a budget. This means handle your money carefully. Some people don't have enough so they have to monitor their money carefully in order to make ends meet. Others have so much that they can easily waste it. Wasting it is poor stewardship of the assets that God has entrusted to our care. A budget keeps both too little or too much well under control.

The Money Trap

A hush descends on my classroom whenever we discuss tithing. Many of the students are thinking rather highly of their spiritual progress until I point out that non-tithers, by definition, are spiritual children. To refuse to obey one of Jesus' commands can only mean that we're still spiritual children. Tithing is one of the few areas where we can actually measure how far along we are in our journey. The record is right in our checkbooks.

In speaking to the Pharisees, Jesus is speaking to us:

> Give God a tenth of your mint, rue, and all other kinds of garden herbs, but you neglect justice and the love of God. You should have practiced the latter (justice and love) without leaving the former (the tithe) undone. (Luke 11:42 NIV)

Spiritual children wonder, "Can I afford to tithe?" Or, "How can I tithe? I'm barely getting by with what I have now." Or," "If I don'ttithe I'll have just enough money to cover the mortgage on a new house." Or, "If I don't tithe, I will have enough money to buy that shiny new car instead of the old plain one that I can afford." Or, "What if I don't have enough left over to make ends meet each month"?

The reason that tithing is so important, is because it is the most powerful tool we have for overcoming the rival god of Materialism.

> *No one can serve two masters. Either he will hate the one and love the other, or he will be devoted to the one and despise the other. You cannot serve both God and Mammon (money).* (Matthew 6:24 NIV)

Let me illustrate. One of my favorite things to do in teaching classes on biblical economics is to have everyone stand up and take out their purse or wallet.

Then, I ask them to exchange their purse or wallet with the person standing next to them. People begin to get anxious.

Then, I ask them to open up the other person's purse or wallet and look inside. People are really nervous.

Then, I say, "Now, were going to take an offering." Most chuckle nervously; some are downright uneasy.

Can you imagine that most in the class are more concerned about what happens to their money than they are about the Bible lesson for the morning! Such is the rival god.

When I got my first paycheck, my dad said, "You start, right now; take ten percent of everything you ever make and tithe it. You do that and God promises that He will meet every need you will ever have." So, I've tithed on every dollar that I ever earned, and Jesus has met my every need.

The only time in the Bible that God invites us to test him is in regard to tithing.

Will a man rob God? Yet you rob me.

But you ask, "How do we rob you?"

> *In tithes and offerings. You are under a curse the whole nation of you—because you are robbing me.*
>
> *"Bring the whole tithe into the storehouse, that there may be food in my house. Test me in this," says the LORD Almighty, "and see if I will not throw open the floodgates of heaven and*

pour out so much blessing that you will not have room enough for it. (Malachi 3:8-12 NIV)

It is not possible to go on to maturity while mismanaging God's money.

By the way again, the usual restaurant tip is fifteen percent. It is rude to leave less. God only asks for ten percent, so I wonder what some Christians are griping about.

Spiritual children usually spend everything they make on themselves. So, when they finally decide to tithe, tithe they are so overspent that they literally have no money to give.

For some it's right to take the plunge and start tithing immediately.

I advise other individuals to start small—like 2%--and build up judiciously until they reach 10%. This takes self-discipline and a budget.

As God processes us with the cross of sanctification, we learn that we can depend upon God—at any price. Spiritual mothers and fathers settled the tithing issue long ago.

Evangelism

Evangelism comes naturally to spiritual mothers and fathers. It is part of their job description.

However, for new Christians, the best time for them to evangelize is shortly after their new birth. As new Christians, spiritual children usually have a host of friends who need Jesus.

Unfortunately, as newborn babies grow up, they tend to have more and more Christian friends and less and less friends who don't know Jesus. The newborn babies now go to church, attend Bible studies, and get involved in all sorts of Christian activities. As new Christians surround themselves with more Christian friends, their pool of friends who don't know Jesus begins to shrink dramatically.

I was so excited about being a Christian that I told my two best friends, Jim and Billy, so that they could be Christians, too. When Billy's mother heard me talking about Jesus, she made me stop. On the other hand, Jim and I were baptized together several Sunday nights later. Jim died in a car wreck when he was 17 years old. Glad he's in heaven!

Christians are responsible to share the gospel whatever their spiritual level may be.

> *We are therefore Christ's ambassadors, as though God were making his appeal through us. We implore you on Christ's behalf: Be reconciled to God.* (2 Corinthians 5:20 NIV)

Beliefs and Doctrines

Spiritual children struggle often with their beliefs and doctrines. The Apostle Paul explains that spiritual children are most susceptible to being ...

> *... tossed back and forth by the waves . . . blown here and there by every wind of teaching and by the cunning and craftiness of men in their deceitful scheming.* (Ephesians 4:13-14 NIV)

Spiritual children are easily seduced by false teachings. For example, a Mormon missionary comes to the door and says something that soundsl biblical. The spiritual child, who doesn't know the Word of God very well, swallows what he or she hears, and responds, "I didn't know that Jesus and Adam were brothers!" The hook is set.

The gospel of Christ taught by Paul in Romans and Galatians is extremely different from the teachings of the Mormon Church. Paul taught that faith plus "nothing" provides for salvation.

The Mormon religion inserts numerous things that must be accomplished if one is to be saved. Paul is careful to clarify that salvation is a free gift that we can never earn. In fact, Paul says that if we try to earn salvation, we lose it:

> *For it is by grace you have been saved, through faith—and this not from yourselves, it is the gift of God—not by works, so that no one can boast.* (Ephesians 2:8–9 NIV)

Remaining a spiritual child is dangerous! It's no wonder that Paul, Peter, and the writer to the Hebrews all admonished their readers, "Stop being children—grow up!"

Fear of the World

Spiritual children tend to be fearful and insecure. Fear and insecurity often spring from a lack of faith.

Most young children are scared of the dark at bedtime: "I'm afraid to go to sleep. Monsters are in the closet! Alligators are under the bed!"

I had the same kind of fears when I was a child. I often dreamed that I was one of the Three Little Pigs and we were riding in the back of a garbage truck racing down the alley with the Big Bad Wolf close behind. But now I am grown up. The Big Bad Wolf hasn't chased me in quite a while.

We all know how to handle our children when they are afraid. We put them on our knee and reason with them. "Was there any water on the floor when you walked in?"

"No, daddy."

"Well then, there can't be an alligator under the bed. How about monsters in the closet? Did you hear the alarm system go off?"

"No, daddy."

"If there were monsters in the closet our alarm would go off. Do you hear the alarm?"

"No. Thanks dad, I see that I have nothing to worry about. You can leave now; I can go right to sleep."

Is that how it works? Of course not. We hold them and cuddle them and assure them that we'll be right there. You may even sing a song to quiet your child. My dad used to sing, "The nights are long since you went away, and all through the day, my buddy, my buddy, there's no nobody quite like you." I still sometimes sing it today.

Little children struggle with all sorts of fears because many of the experiences necessary to build faith have yet to occur.

In Matthew 14, the storm was raging on the Sea of Galilee. Jesus was asleep in the back of the boat. The disciples awakened Jesus and shouted, "Don't you care that we are going to die?"

Jesus stood up, raised His hands, and commanded the wind and waves to be calmed. Instantly, the storm subsided, and all was well. Then Jesus looked at the frightened men: "You of little faith, why did you doubt?" (Matthew 8:26 NIV).

Was He scolding them? I think not! He was cuddling them! Jesus used a Greek word that can be translated as "Little Faiths, why were you afraid, you little faiths? I'm right there with you."

We don't scold our children for not having enough faith when they face fear and anxiety. We lovingly help them mature into men and women of great faith.

Fear of the Lord

Growing, maturing faith overcomes fear. The concept of biblical fear is often confusing for spiritual children. *"The fear of the Lord is the beginning of wisdom"* (Proverbs 9:10 NIV) must be balanced with the parallel truth in 1 John 4:18: *"There is no fear in love. But perfect love drives out fear, because fear has to do with punishment. The one who fears is not made perfect in love."*

In the early days of the journey, spiritual children do well to fear the Lord. As they mature the "fear of the Lord" morphs into "perfect love that drives out fear." By the way, living in the fear of the Lord is an attractive, healthy way to live.

> *The fear of the Lord is the beginning of wisdom.* (Proverbs 9:10 NIV)
>
> *The fear of the Lord adds length to life,* (Proverbs 10:27 NIV)
>
> *He who fears the Lord has a secure fortress, and for his children it will be a refuge.* (Proverbs 14:26 NIV)
>
> *The fear of the Lord leads to life. Then one rests content, untouched by trouble.* (Proverbs 19:23 NIV)
>
> *The fear of the Lord is a fountain of life, turning a man from the snares of death.* (Proverbs 14:27 NIV)

According to Solomon, then fear of the Lord draws us nearer to God, shaping us into the men and women that He wants us to be.

Children often start out fearing what God might demand of them. As perfect love casts out fear, they can hardly wait to see what God has in store for them.

Throughout my childhood, I lived with a sense of fear of what my mom and dad might do for punishment if I got out of line.

When it was time for discipline, they carefully mixed fear with love. "I am only disciplining you because I love you. I want you to be someone special; I don't want you ever to behave like that again. I love you."

Then they administered appropriate discipline in proportion to the "crime." Fear of discipline from mom and dad was often a factor in some of the decisions that my brother Ronnie and I made as children. My brother and I are the better for it.

Solomon declared that the "fear of Lord is the beginning of wisdom"—*but it is not the end*. The perfect love of God soon drives out the fear. As our love relationship with God grows, our fear dissipates. Think about that as you read the following story.

> *During the Revolutionary War, a young officer in the British Army became engaged to a young lady in England. Then he left for the American colonies.*
>
> *In one of the battles, the officer was badly wounded and lost a leg. He wrote to his fiancée, telling her that he was disfigured and maimed, so changed that he felt that it was his duty to release her from any obligation to become his wife.*
>
> *Can you imagine the threat of rejection and the fear that coursed through the heart of that young officer? He did the honorable thing. But he faced a life alone.*
>
> *In a letter of response, the young lady replied that whether or not they married had nothing whatsoever to do with what had happened to him in battle. She wrote, "I intend to marry you as long as there is enough of your body left to hold your soul!"*

Can you imagine how her "perfect" love drove fear from that soldier's heart? As we mature in our relationship with Jesus, we are able to hear Him say the same thing: "I will love you as long as there is enough of your body left to hold your soul—and long after that as well."

Fights and Altercations

As we grow in our love for God, we sometimes struggle to love each other. Unfortunately, spiritual children occasionally fight with other Christians. Paul confronted this issue in his first letter to the Corinthian church:

*Brothers, I could not address you as spiritual but as worldly—
mere infants in Christ. ... For since there is jealousy and
quarreling among you, are you not worldly? Are you not acting
like mere men?"* (1 Corinthians 3:1-3 NIV)

Julie and I were brokenhearted after we attended our first
denominational convention. As a new pastor, I was excited at the
prospect of spending three days in fellowship and worship with like-
minded Christian workers from all across the world. We'd heard that
power struggles were going on behind the scenes regarding the
direction of our denominational organization, but we were woefully
unprepared for what transpired in the first afternoon session.

A crucial motion was made by one religio-political contingent.
They sought to engineer a takeover in order to ensure that the
domination moved in the direction they wanted.

Meanwhile, buses disgorged thousands of handpicked delegates
outside in the parking lot who were brought in to guarantee the
outcome of the vote. The fighting began as each side accused the
other of ungodly maneuvering. I never knew that Christian leaders
could behave in such unchristian manners. Some of the women near
us began to cry as the shouting and name calling continued.

Julie and I never went back again. We had no desire to be part of
a denomination led by spiritual children.

Hardening Hearts

In 1 Corinthians 3:1-3, Paul was also brokenhearted—in fact rather
angry—over some Corinthian Christians who had decided to remain
spiritual babies.

The first use of the word "worldly" (*sarkinos* in Greek) refers to
smooth, tender, fresh, brand-new skin, baby skin. Paul's point is that
all Christians start out as "fresh-skinned" babies. He characterized
this group as "mere infants in Christ." At this point, if babies drink
spiritual milk, taking in biblical truth, they will begin to mature.

Tragically, some infants have chosen otherwise. Paul described
the second group as "worldly." But this time he used a slightly
different Greek word—*sarkikos*—which has to do with old,
weathered, hardened, and sun-damaged flesh or skin. After plenty
of time to mature, this group of Christians were still in infancy—only
of a twisted sort of hardened infancy.

Have you ever noticed the skin of a man or woman who has spent an inordinate amount of time out in the sun? Before the skin-damaging properties of the ultraviolet rays were widely understood, people actually used to sit out in the sun and "soak up the rays." Now, thirty, forty, or fifty years later, their "fleshly" skin is like leather: hard, dry, and cracking . . . *sarkikos*.

Paul declared that these Christians were now "hardened flesh." Instead of living as spiritual men and women, they were living as spiritually hardened babies.

The warning is clear. Anyone who remains a "fresh-skinned" baby Christian long enough will eventually become hardened. If we don't move deliberately forward in our spiritual journey, we are in grave danger of becoming hard to mold into the image of Christ.

How long can we remain as fresh-skinned children before we begin to harden?

My guess is three years. Why three years? Jesus's disciples were trained and ready after three years of discipleship. Paul spent three years teaching the Ephesian church the "whole counsel of God" (see Acts 20:27). When he departed, he called all the elders together and declared them ready to carry on the ministry in Ephesus. Though this is just an estimate, I would argue that the biblical precedent is clear.

Peter Pan, the children's tale by Sir James M. Barrie is a fictional story of a boy who refused to grow up. Peter Pan the boy makes for a charming story.[16] But Peter Pan, the man or the woman who will not grow up, is a tragedy.

Moving to the Next Stage

As I close this lesson, the most frequently asked questions from my students are, "How can we know that we are spiritually mature? How will we know that we have finally arrived?" Others ask, "What if I don't make it to full maturity as spiritual mother/father? Does that mean we are losers? Is there some goal line we have to cross to achieve the level of mother or father? Is that when God considers us winners?"

The answers are simple. The journey to maturity is never completed while we're here on earth. When we finally reached the mountaintops, we see that there are more peaks ahead. We'll only be fully like Christ when we get to heaven.

So, we set our hearts on growing up in Christ . . . and someday when we least expect it, we will realize that we are no longer children;

we've grown into spiritual young men and women; and eventually, spiritual mothers and fathers.

Father,

I want to delight in You like Asaph did in Psalm 73: "Whom have I in heaven but you? And being with you, I desire nothing on earth." Move me forward in my spiritual journey. Help me to recognize any tendencies or habits that are holding me back. Please help me mature as a spiritual mother/father at any price.

Amen.

CHAPTER 4

SPIRITUAL YOUNG MEN AND WOMEN

Spiritual young men and women exercise their spiritual muscles, learning from the Word of God (both Jesus and the Bible) and fighting Satan on his own ground and winning.
"I write to you, young men, because you are strong, and the word of God lives in you, and you have overcome the evil one." 1 John 2:14 (NIV)

Sally sat before me, her face etched with pain. Nerves damaged by radiation treatments kept this deacon's wife in constant agony. "The doctors say they can do nothing more," she said to me. "God is my only hope. I noticed a passage on healing in James 5:14-16 I thought might help. Would you please gather the elders and pray for me?"

Unfortunately, it was not that simple. Our denominational church traditions did not allow for personal healing services as outlined in James 5:14-16:

> *"Is anyone among you sick? Let them call the elders of the church to pray over them and anoint them with oil in the name of the Lord. And the prayer offered in faith will make the sick person well; the Lord will raise them up. If they have sinned, they will be forgiven. Therefore confess your sins to each*

other and pray for each other so that you may be healed. The prayer of a righteous person is powerful and effective."

Furthermore, I was not sure what the "prayer offered in faith" really was. I had never anointed anyone with oil before. As a young pastor, I was scared and uncertain. However, I had recently begun practicing the discipline of fasting, and I knew one purpose of fasting was to find God's will.

I explained my pastoral dilemma to Sally and then proposed a solution: "I suggest we both pray and fast for five days. I'll meet you in my office next Friday afternoon, and if God tells us to proceed, we will." Sally was no novice. She had walked with God for many years. She agreed to the proposal.

Five days later, we both wrote down what we thought God was telling us and then exchanged papers. Our conclusions were identical. We made plans for a healing service on Sunday afternoon. Since our church policies did not allow for elders (we had deacons), I arranged for our deacons to attend. I figured deacons would be a suitable substitute in light of our circumstances.

During the 30 minutes before Sally arrived, I explained her request to our leaders, the background of her medical condition, and what I knew of James 5:14-16. When I asked if anyone had participated in a healing service before, no hands rose. We were entering uncharted territory.

When Sally arrived, we asked her to confess any known sins that might relate to her sickness (because James mentioned this in verse 16). When she finished, I took the bottle of olive oil I had purchased at the supermarket and prepared to pour oil over her head. One of the deacons averted a mess when he shook his head and gestured that a drop on a finger applied lightly to her forehead might work better. We took turns passing the bottle, anointing her with oil, and praying for her.

I wondered if Sally would leap up and shout, "Glory to God! I'm healed!" like I'd seen on television. But she did not. In fact, nothing happened. She thanked us for our prayers and left a room full of disappointed deacons.

Unknown to us, the healing service simply moved to another time and place. In the early morning hours, Sally was awakened by a strange sensation of warmth moving down her spine. She knew instantly she had been healed. By the time she got out of bed, the pain was gone.

Later Sally shared an intriguing observation: "I think the reason God didn't heal me yesterday afternoon was because all of you men might have become proud. I think God waited until I was alone so He would get all the glory." She never had another pain as long as she lived. I buried her many years later.

Fasting is one of the spiritual disciplines. When properly used, spiritual disciplines not only allow the power of God to flow, they also increase God-dependence with a corresponding decrease in self-reliance, self-centeredness, and self-condemnation. Spiritual young men and women grow strong by practicing the spiritual disciplines.

Exercising Muscles

Let's begin with "young men are strong." The Greek word for "strong," (*ischuros*) refers to the spiritual power that develops as a result of our progressively deepening relationship with Jesus, as well as our expanding knowledge of the content of the Bible.

When I look out over the men and women in my spiritual growth classes, I don't usually see a lot of big, physical muscles. There are some strong, muscular people in our midst—just not many. How did they get those big muscles? There are no secrets here. They lift weights and exercise. At the fitness center, the trainers say, "Lift these weights repeatedly, and you will develop big, strong muscles. Follow these exercises, and you'll get stronger." It takes a great deal of discipline and effort to build big muscles. However, anybody can do it if they want to.

My experience is that most Christians never develop big, strong spiritual muscles. They seldom exercise their faith, perhaps because they don't know how. However, there are no secrets here. Spiritual disciplines are God-given spiritual exercises to build strong spiritual muscles.

The spiritual disciplines are biblical activities recognized throughout Christian history as essential for reaching spiritual maturity. They include celebration, confession, fellowship, fasting, meditation, prayer, Bible study, service, **evangelism, worship,** disciple making, generosity, solitude, simplicity, and **stewardship.**

The disciplines produce humility, brokenness, spiritual power, and a corresponding decrease in self-reliance, self-centeredness, and self-condemnation. God's strength is what we want to experience—not our own. Remember, the victory belongs to God and not to us.

The Bible teaches that fasting has multiple purposes. For example, fasting is useful for finding God's will, for guaranteeing safety in traveling, for changing God's mind when used in conjunction with repentance, for petitioning God for healing, and for exorcising demonic spirits, among other things.

Developing our own spiritual gifts is another way by which we build strong spiritual muscles. By God's design, our most profitable service will be in exercising the specific spiritual gifts given to us by the Holy Spirit at the time of our conversion.

We serve the body of Christ by discovering and employing our spiritual gifts in a manner that helps others grow to maturity. As we utilize our gifts, our productivity for the kingdom increases dramatically.

The spiritual gifts are found in three separate passages in the New Testament: Romans 12; 1 Corinthians 12-14; and Ephesians 4. The lists are not identical. Some overlap occurs. Every Christian is given at least one gift at conversion. Our initial gift may lie dormant for a while as we mature. We might call these early impartations "driving force" gifts. They remain with us throughout our ministry lives.

Other spiritual gifts may be thought of in terms of a toolbox full of tools. At times, God may utilize a particular gift on a short-term basis in order to minister to a particular need in the body of Christ. As we manage well our initial gifts, and as our ministries expand, we may ask God for other gifts under the direction of the inner promptings of the Holy Spirit (see 1 Corinthians 14).

I would be remiss if I failed to mention that we become strong by solidifying the beliefs, values, morals, and relationships that characterize the Christian life.

The Word of God

The term "Word of God" in the Gospel of John refers to Jesus Christ on the one hand and to the Bible on the other. John's Gospel begins: *"In the beginning was the Word, and the Word was with God, and the Word was God." John 1:1 (NIV)* In verse 14, he declared: *"The Word became flesh and made his dwelling among us. We have seen his glory, the glory of the one and only Son, who came from the Father, full of grace and truth." (NIV)*

"Word" is the English translation of the Greek word, *logos*. John used this Greek philosophical term to refer to the unrevealed wisdom of God. John declared that at a point in time the unrevealed wisdom of God put on a human body and lived on earth for all to see.

Not only had the *Logos* become flesh, at the moment of our new birth the living Lord Jesus indwelt our bodies. Spiritual young men and women are beginning to manifest the heart of the Lord Jesus. This transformation should come as no surprise; after all, we are indwelt by the living Word of God: *"Christ in you, the hope of glory."* *Colossians 1:27 (NIV)*

His life is the real source that enables us to grow strong. Out of our deepening relationship with Jesus, spiritual young men and women develop the mind of Christ (see Philippians 2:1–12), so it is no surprise that we begin to look and act a lot like Christ.

Jesus is the spoken Word; the Bible is the written Word. Not only do young men and women master the content of the Bible, they become skilled at making relevant, practical applications for themselves and others. They learn to impart godly guidance and direction by bringing the Bible to bear upon the problems, issues, and struggles in people's lives.

By definition, those Christians who do not know the Word of God well, and how to apply it wisely, are still spiritual children.

How well do you know the Bible? For some of us, this is a soul-searching question.

In my spiritual growth class, I often ask the students to outline the book of Philippians in four sentences. Only a few can do it, if any. This task isn't hard—the book has only four chapters, and each is easily summarized in one sentence.

Are you aware that two Psalms are alike? Those who spend any significant time reading the Psalms will notice that Psalms 14 and 53 are basically identical. Why were they both included?

What Bible book is just like Ephesians? Try Colossians.

The book of Jude resembles what other New Testament book? We can't read Jude without wondering at its similarities to 2 Peter.

This is not Bible trivia. If we spend any quality time at all in the Bible, we will observe these things. Most of my students fail miserably.

Hebrews is really the fifth gospel. Why? Which Old Testament Book is the best commentary on Hebrews? Hebrews is incomprehensible without a working knowledge of Leviticus.

Can you sum up the book of Obadiah in one word? Obadiah is only one page long. Imagine walking down the streets of heaven and running into Obadiah:

"Hi, I'm Obadiah."

"Didn't you write a book in the Bible?"

"Yes, how did you like it?"

"Uh . . . uh . . . I never read it."

What's the only one of Jesus' miracles recorded in all four Gospels? Answer: The feeding of the five thousand. What happened next? And why then?

These are not frivolous questions. If we are going to shepherd little lambs, we must know the content of the Bible so we can apply the Word for their profit and edification. When we become spiritual young men and women, our knowledge of the Bible further enhances our shepherding role.

By the way, my favorite Bible book when I have trouble sleeping is Leviticus. Why? Go read Leviticus and you'll see why.

Some of you are tempted to say, "Roger, this is too hard. You are asking too much!"

First of all, I'm not the One who is asking. Knowing and applying the content of the Bible is God's plan for maturity.

Second, it is not that hard. We are not talking about mastering the Word in two or three years. For most of us, our long-term spiritual processing as young men and women requires 15 to 20-plus years of development. A little bit of Bible study every day or so adds up to quite a lot in 15 or 20 years.

Spiritual young men and women know the words of God are bread and life. They meet God on the pages of Scripture.

Overcoming Satan

Spiritual young men and women understand the strategies and tactics of spiritual warfare. They know how to beat Satan at his own game.

Spiritual children on the other hand are often duped into thinking either the world of demonic spiritual forces doesn't exist or, if it does exist, the demonic forces have so little interaction with our lives they can summarily be dismissed. Spiritual children are easily tricked into thinking everything spiritual comes from God. So, they often miss the deceptive workings of Satan and can fall prey to all sorts of satanic counterfeits.

On the other hand, spiritual, young men and women have enough experience to know not every spirit comes from God. They become skilled in knowing what is of God—and what is not.

The most dangerous moment in our spiritual lives may well be the moment we decide to go on to maturity at any price. I guarantee that Satan will offer a counterfeit. He offered one in the Garden of Eden. "Do you want to be like God?" "Certainly!" He baited the hook and Adam and Eve swallowed it. He neglected to tell them the part about becoming like Satan instead of becoming like God.

Spiritual young men and women are wary lest Satan seduce them into a kind of life that is not the life of Christ at all.

For example, the second century heretical Gnostics believed they alone had received special wisdom from God. Therefore, they were on a higher level than other Christians. This is a far cry from Paul's teaching in Philippians, *"I want to know Christ—yes, to know the power of his resurrection and participation in his sufferings." Philippians 3:10 (NIV)*

One of our ushers sat frightened in my office. He had foolishly attended a worship service at a spiritualist church. Why in the world he prayed to receive a "spirit guide" I will never understand—except that he was still a spiritual child.

While he related several recent spiritual manifestations, he stopped speaking and settled into a trance. I was getting scared as I watched in fascination. Several moments later, he shook his head and asked, "They were back, weren't they?" I understand now he was under a satanic attack.

I confirmed something unusual had happened, but neither of us knew what "they" were. Fortunately, I had recently finished reading *The Adversary*[17] by Mark Bubeck. I gave our usher a copy: "Here, read this. Follow his guidance and pray the appropriate written prayers. I believe you will find freedom." He did.

One of my favorite instructional books on the game of golf is *How to Play Your Best Golf All of the Time*[18], by Tommy Armour. It comes as close as humanly possible to teaching someone how to play golf without ever hitting a golf ball. But no one has ever learned to play golf from reading a book. No one has ever learned to play tennis or how to swim from reading a book. We have to pick up a golf club. We have to pick up a racket. We have to get into the water.

In the same way, no one ever learned how to fight spiritual battles by just reading the Bible. We have to experience the war. We must actually fight.

I pastored a small, rural church during my college years. Richard, one of the fine Christian men in our church, suffered a massive heart attack and was in a coma. On Thursday, Julie and I went to the hospital to encourage his wife, Jane. It was lunchtime, so we offered to sit with her husband while she took a break.

Richard was unconscious. Julie and I decided to pray for him. About five minutes into our prayer, Richard uttered, "Jesus Christ did not come in the flesh."

Startled, I looked at Julie; she looked at me. We both knew 1 John 4:2-3:

> "This is how you can recognize the Spirit of God: Every spirit that acknowledges that Jesus Christ has come in the flesh is from God, but every spirit that does not acknowledge Jesus is not from God. This is the spirit of the antichrist, which you have heard is coming and even now is already in the world." 1 John 4:2-3 (NIV)

"Roger" Julie whispered, "Did he say, 'Jesus Christ did not come in the flesh'?"

"I think so!"

"Do you think he has a demonic spirit of antichrist?"

"I wouldn't think so."

Just that morning in my "Life and Teachings of Christ" class, the professor taught about Jesus' encounter with the Gadarene demoniac. I looked at Julie and said, "Dr. Flanders said whenever Jesus confronted a demon, He first found out the demon's name. If this is a demon, let's pray for it to reveal its name."

We had no idea what we were doing! We held hands, bowed our heads, touched his shoulders, and prayed, "If this is a demonic spirit, we demand in the name of Jesus Christ, by the blood of Jesus Christ, that you reveal your name!"

Our comatose friend moved his lips to pronounce the words, "My name is Clarissus."

"Clarissus?!?" His name was Richard! Julie took a deep breath and asked, "What do we do now?"

"I don't know! The dismissal bell rang before Dr. Flanders finished the lecture. All I know is that Jesus cast that demon into some pigs! Should we pray for the demon to come out?"

We resumed positions and prayed . . . nothing happened. After a while, Jane returned.

"Well, how'd it go?" she asked.

I looked at Julie; she looked at me. "Fine," I lied. We were afraid she would think we were crazy!

Julie and I were in the parking lot when Jane ran out of the hospital lobby, yelling, "What happened in there? What happened in there?"

I looked at Julie; she looked at me. "Um . . . nothing . . . we just prayed for Richard."

"Well," she said, "he has this big smile on his face. Something happened in there!"

About ten o'clock that night, Richard regained consciousness, opened his eyes, and said to Jane, "I had the strangest dream. I was climbing up the steps to heaven, and when I got to the gate, Peter said, 'You can't come in now.' So, I climbed back down the steps. I guess this means God has some special things left for me to do."

Ten minutes later, Richard had another massive coronary. I buried him three days later.

Questions spun in my mind as we laid him to rest. The answers I wanted were buried with him.

When I was 19 years old, I began to pray, "Dear Jesus, please make me a spiritual man at any price," I never imagined this might include "overcoming the evil one."

In the ensuing years, I've fought numerous spiritual battles with some exhilarating victories and many heartbreaking defeats. I've found that battles with Satan and his forces are seldom overt. Most

Christians will never have an encounter like the one we had with Clarissus. Most spiritual battles are won by consistent discipleship and by utilizing the biblical tools God has already placed at our disposal.

The Apostle John wrote of spiritual young men and women, "You have overcome the evil one." 1 John 2:14 (NIV) The word "overcome" means to "conquer," to "master," to "prevail over," to "make helpless," to "overpower," or to "overwhelm." John meant that spiritual young men and women know how to engage Satan and his demons in hand-to-hand spiritual combat and win!

In another sense, the word "overcome" means to no longer be deceived by Satan's workings and devices. Satan's basic work against Christians is accomplished with lies and deceit. His basic tools are temptations, accusations, and insinuations.

Remember how Satan tried to overcome Job. The test between God and Satan concerned whether Satan could get Job to curse God. The evil one tried to sneak in the back door of Job's life by deceiving Job's wife into tempting him to "curse God and die." In fact, Job was deceived throughout the entire book. He thought God was the author of all the mischief in his life. He never saw the satanic struggle which was going on behind the scenes.

Spiritual young men and women are no longer deceived by the workings of the evil one. Not only can they defend themselves adequately in battle, they help those who have been ensnared in his traps.

Sometimes spiritual battle is the only way to get enough experience to take on the evil one.

I recall early my ministry a grandmother coming to my office for counseling. She was terrified as she told me demons were after her and were going to kill her. I did not know what to do with that. I thought she must be crazy!

However, early the next morning I got a phone call from her granddaughter. She said, "Grandmother slipped in the bathtub this morning and her head hit the faucet as she fell. The paramedics are here, but there is no doubt she is dead."

Several days later I performed her funeral service.

That experience was a learning time for me.

Demonic encounters must be kept in proper perspective. As the deliverance ministry emerged as part of our counseling center, we discovered almost all demonic problems were discipleship issues. Direct intervention was rarely needed. Most Christians will never face such a dramatic occurrence. Fortunately, every tool we need for victory is provided in the written Word of God.

We need to keep our spiritual eyes and ears open. We don't want to be deceived like Job.

I am convinced that anyone who sits through a deliverance session and observes a woman from Mexico who speaks only Spanish converse in clear English while under the manifestation of demonic spirits will become an instant believer in the power and reality of the evil one.

Of course, there are biblical precedents for the story I just told. The disciples were certainly believers when they joyfully returned from a mission and excitedly reported to Jesus, *"Even the demons submit to us in your name!" Luke 10:17 (NIV)*

> Jesus replied, *"Do not rejoice that the spirits submit to you, but rejoice that your names are written in heaven." Luke 10:20 (NIV)*

This is a good time to point out why very little overt demonic action is seen in developed countries. We hear about many demonic struggles, visions and miracles occurring in developing countries, but not in Europe and North America. Why?

Satan doesn't need use his big guns in developed countries, because developed countries are mired in materialism. (See Matthew 6:24.)

Someone in my class always, always, says at this point: "I want to be a spiritual mother (or father) someday; but I don't want to deal with this Satan stuff. It scares me. Can I be a spiritual mother (or father) and skip this part?"

No.

Servants

Jesus described Himself as a servant and urged all His followers to serve one another. One demonstration that men and women are growing toward maturity is an others-centered mentality. Paul describes this in Philippians:

> "In humility value others above yourselves, not looking to your own interests but each of you to the interests of the others." Philippians 2:3-4 (NIV)

The Apostle Paul connected serving one another to the Great Commandment:

> *"You, my brothers and sisters, were called to be free. But do not use your freedom to indulge the flesh; rather, serve one another humbly in love. For the entire law is fulfilled in keeping this one command: 'Love your neighbor as yourself.'"* Galatians 5:13–14 (NIV)

The Grace of Giving

Developing a generous heart is a tough challenge. Our natural bent toward selfishness gets in the way. However, generosity is one of God's defining attributes.

> *"Give generously to them and do so without a grudging heart; then because of this the Lord your God will bless you in all your work and in everything you put your hand to."* Deuteronomy 15:10 (NIV)
>
> *Paul encourages us in this:*
>
> *"But since you excel in everything—in faith, in speech, in knowledge, in complete earnestness and in the love we have kindled in you—see that you also excel in this grace of giving."* 2 Corinthians 8:7 (NIV)

As we mature into the image of Christ, we grow more and more in the grace of giving. We give from our resources to meet one another's financial needs.

Remember that one characteristic of spiritual children is they still think the money they have is theirs and not God's. Spiritual young men and women develop and integrate good financial planning, so they don't spend everything they make on themselves. They always have a surplus to be able to help the needs of others. Spiritual young men and women understand they are managers and not owners.

Each day my daughter Jessie remained in the hospital pushed Julie and me deeper into financial distress. The bills climber higher and faster than our bank account and insurance reimbursements. After she died, all the bills came due. Kind people at Casas Church took up a love offering to help. Then we emptied the only bank account we had, and we still came up short by almost $2,000.

Merle, one of our church members, invited me out to lunch shortly after the love offering was given at church. After we ordered our food, he reached in his coat pocket and pulled out his checkbook. "How much are you short?"

"What do you mean?"

"I know you have a lot of bills; I know how much the offering was, and I know insurance rarely covers enough. I want to know how much you need."

"Well, the best Julie and I can figure, we are about $1,800 short."

Merle started to write out a check. He caught me totally off guard. "Wait a minute," I stammered, "I can't let you do that."

"Sure you can. God has given Bonnie and me the resources. You have the need. What else would you expect us to do?"

As he handed the check to me across the table, he looked me in the eye and said firmly, "If any more bills come in, they are mine."

Spiritual Pride

The fact that we are growing spiritually, but are not yet spiritual mothers and fathers, often manifests as pride. Paul acknowledges this in 1 Corinthians:

> *"Knowledge puffs up while love builds up. Those who think they know something do not yet know as they ought to know." 1 Corinthians 8:1-2 (NIV)*

I wanted to be the best pastor God ever had. I imagined walking through St. Peter's gate and hearing God say, "Oh, Roger, you're finally here! You were the best pastor I ever had! You did things Moses never did!" Is this not pure, unadulterated, ugly pride? I thought growing a big church made me a great pastor.

I was "puffing up." I had a little knowledge and a little experience, and I thought I was ready to go out and win the whole world for Jesus. It's easier to "puff up" than to "love up."

In 1 Corinthians 8, Paul addressed one of the problems that often occurs among Christ-followers who are at different levels of spiritual maturity. He instructed the stronger Christians to yield their freedom in Christ so as not to offend the consciences of their weaker brothers and sisters in Christ. After yielding, the stronger are to help the weaker develop their own freedom in Christ. This often means we help to retrain the consciences of weaker brothers to become more biblically centered.

If we are not careful, pride in our knowledge will lead us into a ministry of condemnation rather than a ministry of loving edification.

Encouragement For the Journey

As I close this lesson in my classroom, I always try to encourage my students with a litany of biblical heroes who were orphaned, abandoned, fatherless, homeless, or otherwise suffered through tremendous struggles during their teenage years.

Joseph was rejected by his brothers and sold into slavery in Egypt as a teenager. When Potiphar's wife made sexual advances, Joseph did not compromise his integrity. Falsely accused by her, he was imprisoned. But prison later opened the door to an audience with the Pharaoh.

Daniel was carried off to Babylon, 600 miles from home when he was only 14 years old. He was tempted to give up on his God and bow down and worship a pagan god. His risky refusal was honored by God. Daniel became a trusted advisor to King Nebuchadnezzar. At the age of 95, he transcended empires.

Esther was 16 when she entered Xerxes' harem. Through God's providential intervention, she became aware of a plot to destroy all the Jews in Persia. She alone could stand against the treachery. By crossing the king's doorway uninvited, she placed her life in jeopardy. But she said fearlessly, "If I perish, I perish," and stepped across the threshold. The king smiled; she lived; and a nation of Jews was spared. She was just 16!

God said to Jeremiah, "Be my prophet."

"But I'm just 17."

"That's fine. You're not too young."

Luke observed, *"And Jesus grew in wisdom and stature, and in favor with God and man." Luke 2:52 (NIV)* That verse summarizes 18 years of Christ's life. Even before He was a teenager—at the age of 12—He amazed the elders in the temple with His wisdom and knowledge.

May the same be said of us during our maturing years as spiritual young men and women.

Father,

I know You're deeply interested in my spiritual development and growth. I want to be the spiritual man (or woman) you've designed me to be. Please place within me a hungering desire to mature both in my spiritual life and in my relationship with you.

Please make me a spiritual mother or father at any price.

Amen.

CHAPTER 5

SPIRITUAL MOTHERS AND FATHERS

Spiritual mothers and fathers care for God's flock while enjoying an intimate relationship with Jesus.

Near the end of World War II, a battle occurred in German-occupied France. An American soldier was killed. His comrades wanted to bury his body. They saw a little church down the road and went inside to ask if they could bury their friend in that little church graveyard. The priest asked, "Was your friend a Catholic?"

"No."

"I'm really sorry, but this is a Catholic church, and this is a Catholic graveyard."

So, downhearted, they stepped just outside the cemetery fence, dug a grave, and laid their friend to rest.

The next morning, they received orders to leave the area. They returned to the church for one parting farewell. However, they couldn't find the grave. Finally, they knocked on the church door and said to the priest, "Can you help us? We know we buried our buddy yesterday just outside this fence. But we can't find his grave.

The priest replied, "I sat up the first part of the night feeling sorry for what I said to you. I spent the second part of the night moving the fence."

Spiritual mothers and fathers have a marvelous way of moving the fences and making us one.

Shepherds

Spiritual parents partner with Jesus in the care and nurture of others. Jesus used many metaphors to describe Himself. But He loved best to think of Himself as a shepherd. The crowds in Galilee reminded Him of sheep without a shepherd. He was sent to save the lost sheep of the house of Israel. He pictured Himself one day separating sheep from goats. He said, "I know every sheep by name." He declared, "The good shepherd lays down His life for the sheep." John 10:11 (NIV)

Jesus chose to give this same title of shepherd to Peter when He commissioned him to establish the church: "Feed my lambs . . . Take care of my sheep . . . Feed my sheep." John 21:15-17 (NIV)

The history of the Christian church began with Jesus saying to the leader who was to head up the work of disciplining the nations: "I am a shepherd, you be a shepherd, too." As we mature spiritually, we join with Jesus in shepherding those under our care and in searching for the lost sheep who need a Savior.

The Cycle

Hinds Feet on High Places[19] by Hannah Hurnard is an allegory of the spiritual journey we take in order to mature to look like Jesus. The central character is a young girl named Much Afraid, who lives in the Valley of Humiliation with her family, the Fearings. She wants to travel to the spiritual High Places and to experience the true love of the Shepherd. "Hind" is a British word for a female deer.

Unfortunately, Much Afraid has crooked feet and a twisted mouth. Her cousins Craven Fear, Bitterness, Spiteful, Gloomy, and even her Aunt Dismal Forebodings all unite to stymie her journey. However, the call of the Shepherd was strong. In a moment of supreme courage, aided by other Christ-followers, she left her fearing family behind and ran to find the Shepherd.

Because of her twisted, crippled feet, the Shepherd provided two companions to help her over the rough spots. First, the Shepherd introduced her to Suffering. Much Afraid touched Suffering's hand. It was cold, and she pulled back, saying, "I don't want her."

"The other companion I have selected for you is Sorrow,"

Much Afraid reached out and touched the hand of Sorrow. It was also cold. She pulled back again and said, "I don't want her either!"

The Shepherd replied, "Suffering and Sorrow are the guides best able to lead you to the High Places. I selected them just for you." So, with their help, Much Afraid began her journey.

When she finally reached the High Places, her twisted mouth was straightened, and her crippled feet were healed. She leapt for joy as Sorrow was transformed into Joy and Suffering was transformed into Peace. Much Afraid was transformed into Grace and Glory.

Near the end of the book, Grace and Glory looked down on the high places upon the Valley of Humiliation far below. She thought about her family living in misery. They needed the Shepherd, too! She began to weep, asking Joy and Peace, "What about my family? What will become of them? Who will go and help them?"

Joy replied, "If the Shepherd can turn Sorrow into Joy, and Suffering into Peace, and Much Afraid into Grace and Glory, then the Shepherd can transform Dismal Foreboding into Praise and Thanksgiving. He can do a marvelous work with Craven Fear, Spiteful, Gloomy, and all the other cousins you have down there."

"But who will go? Who is going to tell them?"

She turned to the Shepherd and began to plead, "Can't you send somebody? Who will help my family?"

A smile creased the Shepherd's face. He looked deep into her eyes and said, "Why, that is your job. That is why I brought you here. Now, go back to the valley and lead your family. I want them on the high places, too." [20]

The story of her descent down into the Valley and the transformation of her cousins is told in Hurnard's sequel, *Mountains of Spices*[20]. I was sitting on an airplane at the end of runway 11, waiting to take off from Tucson International Airport, when I finished the sequel. Tears were streaming down my cheeks. Finally, the passenger next to me asked, "Are you all right?"

"Yes, it's just a great book."

This is the essence of the spiritual growth cycle. We start out as children; we grow to be young men and women; we mature as mothers and fathers. Then we descend back down into the valley and help others on their journey to the High Places.

Evangelism

Spiritual mothers and fathers guide lost sheep into the kingdom of God. This is the essence of evangelism. Does that mean we must give birth to be a parent? Yes and no. By definition, parents are those who have given birth to children. Spiritual fathers and mothers give birth to spiritual babies when they lead people to Christ. However, on the other hand, babies may find Christ in other ways. Some find Christ by reading the Bible. Some surrender after hearing the gospel in church, or on the radio, or watching a friend who has recently found Christ.

Sadly, some are spiritually abandoned by those who led them to Christ. These orphans need adoption. Adopting those without parents is the responsibility of spiritual mothers and fathers.

Feeding and Sharing

Mothers and fathers feed spiritual children and young men and women with the Word of God. We teach them basic Christian doctrines. We teach morals and values and character development. We model how to pray, fast, worship, study the Bible, and confess sins. We help our spiritual children discover their spiritual gifts. We help them discern the will of God.

Spiritual mothers and fathers prepare their children for spiritual life. If the job is done right, spiritual parents soon have spiritual grandchildren!

Spiritual parents open up and share their lives. If all we do is teach the Bible, then we have only taught them half the message. Sharing our lives is the other half of the message. We haven't finished our job until we have shared with them the whole gospel – the Word of God and ourselves as well.

> *"Just as a nursing mother cares for her children, so we cared for you. Because we loved you so much, we were delighted to share with you not only the gospel of God but our lives as well." 1 Thessalonians 2:7-8 (NIV)*

Intimacy With the Father

In 1 John 2:12-14, John outlined the depth of our intimacy with Jesus. I pause here t ask my students to meditate on this thought: "What does it do to your heart to know God wants to have an intimate relationship with you?" After offering a moment for reflection, I always say, "It feels good, doesn't it?"

Julie and I have been married for a long time. She came into my life on a summer Sunday morning in church. She arrived late--just in time to run to the piano to play and sing before I got up to preach. It was love at first solo. If someone had said to me in those first few weeks, "Do you know Julie Tacker?" I might have responded, "Certainly, I know her." The Greek word "oida" refers to an introductory knowledge of something or a cursory relationship with someone.

Multiple decades later, I not only know her, I experience her. The Greek word "ginosko" describes our intimate relationship today: I'm thinking her thoughts. I'm reading her mind. She's thinking my thoughts. She's reading my mind. I know what makes her laugh. I know what makes her cry. I know her hopes. I know her hurts. Her needs, her strengths, and her weaknesses are open books before me.

Spiritual mothers and fathers experience the fathomless depths of God's heart. They know Him like few others. They have invested years walking closely with Him—experiencing His life, feeling His feelings, and even hurting for Him when He hurts.

I tell my students that one of the marks of growing to maturity is that we can say after ten or 20 years of being a Christian, "I think I am finally beginning to know the heart of God."

A Godly Perspective

Spiritual mothers and fathers view life and experiences from God's perspective. Life looks different from the resurrection side of the cross than it does from the children's side—or from the chasm of suffering in the middle. The view from the mountaintops is quite different from the view from the valley.

During His ministry, Jesus often told His followers He was going to Jerusalem where He would die and return to life. During his earthly ministry they never did figure out what he meant. But after they witnessed the cross and resurrection, everything looked different. On Easter Sunday morning, the events of the past three days suddenly made sense.

In most situations spiritual children say: "What's God's will?" "What's going on?" "What should I do?" "Why did God do this?" "Why did God allow that?" "What He is doing makes no sense." Spiritual mothers and fathers respond differently. When they encounter the same situations, they talk it over with God and begin to get His perspective from the resurrection side. Now, things begin to make eternal sense.

Not Dogmatic

Spiritual mothers and fathers refuse to be dogmatic because of their growing understanding of the fathomless infinitude of God. Spiritual babies and children often have a rather rigid, narrow, arrogant mindset regarding God and the Bible: "I know what the Bible says. I've read it. If you haven't experienced it like I have or see it like I see it, then you are wrong."

> *"Oh, the depth of the riches of the wisdom and knowledge of God! How unsearchable his judgments, and his paths beyond tracing out!" Romans 11:33 (NIV)*

As we climb the mountains of maturity, we discover there are still more mountain peaks to scale. No one can exhaust the infinite depths of God.

Spiritual parents have synthesized truth down to a few essentials: Jesus Christ is God; Jesus was virgin born; He died a substitutionary death on the cross to forgive the sin of the entire world for all time; He rose from the dead; all who believe in Him as their personal Lord and Savior will have their sins forgiven and can cheat death and live forever.

If we get these essentials right, we will be reconciled to God and spend eternity in heaven with Him! Everything else is child's play.

Let me give an example. A nearby pastor discovered some in his congregation were coming to our church for our Sunday night worship service. He asked them not to go, because he was afraid we would confuse them. His church placed a lot more emphasis on utilizing the spiritual gift of tongues than we did.

One morning, I met him walking to his car after he dropped off his daughter at our Christian school. We began to discuss his recent edict. Finally, I said, "You know, one day we may both be on trial for following Jesus and standing before a firing squad. Neither one of us will care about who speaks in tongues and who doesn't." We are now close friends.

How many times have we seen spiritual children argue over their limited experiences with God? Spiritual mothers and fathers seldom join in the fray.

The people who delude themselves into thinking they have a monopoly on understanding God are like the man who wades out into the surf off the California coast, looks up and down the coastline, tastes the water, feels the waves, and cries out gleefully, "I know the Pacific Ocean." At the same time, a man in China wades out three or four yards into the Pacific, makes the same observations, and declares, "You don't know the Pacific. I know the Pacific."

The truth is that both know basically nothing about the Pacific. It's ludicrous for them to start arguing over who best knows the Pacific Ocean! The same goes for spiritual babies and children when they argue about who knows God and His teachings the best.

In the same way, spiritual mothers and fathers understand God is higher, wiser, greater, and infinitely more complex than any human mind can comprehend.

Compassion

In John 9, Jesus was filled with compassion for a man born blind. The disciples, on the other hand, were more interested in arguing about whose sin brought on this affliction. The disciples were seeking to judge. Christ was seeking to love. As we become more intimate with Christ it simply doesn't matter who sinned or why. Each person still needs compassion.

I was leading a conference in San Francisco in the early days of the AIDS epidemic. The medical community was still sorting out how the virus was transmitted. Sex could do it; that was already proven. How about kissing? Or sweat? No one knew.

A young gentleman asked me for an appointment that afternoon. Later on, as we shook hands, I noticed his hands were dripping with sweat. I knew it; he has AIDS! Immediately, I stopped thinking about him. All I could think about was my hand and his sweat.

I hardly moved as he poured out his heart, confessing his illicit sexual lifestyle, wondering if God could ever forgive him and bring healing to his body. All I could think about was getting to the restroom to wash his sweat off my hand. I held my fingers stiffly apart, not wanting to risk pressing any of his sweat into my skin. I ended the session as quickly as possible. The instant he left, I ran to the sink. No compassion that day. All I wanted to do was wash my hands.

As time passed, I met several AIDS victims. I stopped asking, "Who sinned?" I stopped judging them for their sinful lifestyles.

My attitude changed. I saw some who were involved in gay and lesbian lifestyles. But I also met some hemophiliacs and healthcare workers. As I saw the suffering, I thought of Jesus in John 9. "When will you ever stop asking, 'who sinned?' and be moved with compassion for these people?" As time passed, I didn't care how they got it.

Weeping With Jesus

Spiritual parents sense Christ's pain and compassionately minister comfort and understanding to Him.

When spiritual mothers and fathers enter into the "fellowship of His sufferings" (Philippians 3:10 KJV), they have such an intimacy with God that they feel what Jesus feels and hurt when Jesus hurts. They weep for Jesus as he weeps!

Sharing in His sufferings opens the door for true compassion.

We see this demonstrated in the Garden of Gethsemane. He needed comfort from his disciples because he was hurting. They weren't very good comforters. They went to sleep. So God sent angels to comfort Him.

The disciples missed the chance. But can you imagine we have the opportunity to bless God's heart when he is hurting?

> *"Bless the Lord, O my soul: and all that is within me, bless his holy name." Psalm 103:1 (KJV)*

What is it like to bless God's name? The Bible is filled with examples of how God blesses us. We expect that. Here's a verse that tells us we can bless Him – especially when he's hurting.

Late one Christmas Eve night I got a phone call to come to the hospital. Driving home from a party, Mike collided with a drunk driver and was killed instantly. His mom and dad were in the emergency room as physicians were preparing to harvest his organs to give to others in need.

Mom was crying uncontrollably. Dad was in shock.

It's not trite to say that I was feeling their pain. Then, I got to thinking how Jesus must be feeling as he watched these proceedings. There's no doubt he was hurting deeply. Now is a good time to bless Him.

> *Dear Jesus,*
>
> *I know your heart is breaking as you feel the feelings of these suffering parents. I'm sorry you're hurting for them, too. You have been through enough pain and will endure more as the Father's plan is worked out for you. Maybe these moments are just a touch of the coming cross. I'm sorry you're going through this. I'm sorry you have to feel this pain, too.*
>
> *Amen*

Don't you like to imagine that if you were in the Garden that night, you might have responded differently than the disciples? Can you imagine you might have put your arms around Jesus and comforted Him in His hurts? Can you see yourself weeping with Him as He wept, and praying for Him as He prayed? Wouldn't you want to minister to the needs of a hurting Savior? Of course you would.

You might say, "Well, I can't do that. That was a long time ago—and I wasn't there."

Yes, you can. Jesus said:

> *"'I was hungry and you gave me something to eat, I was thirsty and you gave me something to drink, I was a stranger and you invited me in, I needed clothes and you clothed me, I was sick and you looked after me, I was in prison and you came to visit me.'*
>
> *"Then the righteous will answer him, 'Lord, when did we see you hungry and feed you, or thirsty and give you something to drink? When did we see you a stranger and invite you in, or needing clothes and clothe you? When did we see you sick or in prison?' . . .*
>
> *'Truly I tell you, whatever you did for one of the least of these brothers and sisters of mine, you did for me.' Matthew 25:35-40 (NIV)*

Caring for God's children is the same as caring for Jesus Himself.

The Fellowship of His Sufferings

Let's see if we can enter into the pain of Christ's sufferings. As we meditate upon what Jesus felt during the last week of his life, we find ourselves moved with compassion.

At this point, I invite my students to enter with me into the pain of Christ's sufferings. May I invite you to do the same?

I usually have Julie play quiet piano music as I ask my students to close their eyes and meditate reflectively. I lead them through the last week in the life of Jesus.

Maybe you want to turn on some meditative Christian music. Obviously, you can't close your eyes; but you can interact with the words. Don't be in a hurry. Take your time. See how well you can sense the heart of Jesus during His week before the Cross.

I heard David Ferguson of Intimate Life Ministries share some of the following devotional thoughts at a church camp in northern Arizona. He was focusing upon how Jesus felt during the last week of his life.

Less than two weeks before the crucifixion, Mary and Martha sent word to Jesus their brother, Lazarus was sick. When Jesus finally arrived in Bethany, Lazarus had been dead for four days (John 11). Notice that the main street of Bethany was lined with mourners.

Martha was the first to greet Him. "Lord," she said, "if you had been here, my brother would not have died." I wonder how much hurt and anger echoed in her words: "Where were you? You should have been here! We sent for you four days ago. What were you doing? Lazarus was one of your best friends. I know he'll be resurrected one day; but we wish he were here now."

Have you ever considered that her accusing words stung His sensitive heart?

On the other hand, when Mary heard Jesus had come, she ran to kneel at His feet. She said essentially the same thing as Martha, but the Greek construction she used implied a little different approach. She may well have said something like this: "If you had been here, my brother would not have died. But it's all right; we will all see him again in the resurrection."

Then follows the shortest, most easily remembered verse in the whole Bible: *"Jesus wept." John 11:35 (NIV)*

I used to wonder why He was crying. After all, He knew Lazarus would soon live again. As I closed my eyes and meditated upon the scene, I saw Mary's tears and the weeping of all their friends. Then I understood that the sensitive Savior was moved deeply with compassion, not just for Lazarus, but for all the other mourners as well.

Not long afterward, Jesus was enjoying dinner in the home of Mary, Martha, and Lazarus. Suddenly, Mary violated the Jewish tradition of the day by bursting into the room and anointing Jesus with a bottle of expensive perfume.

Picture Jesus however you like; homespun robe; long, flowing, chestnut-colored hair, parted in the middle; olive skin; sandals on His feet.

Do you see the look of loving adoration on Mary's face as she gazes intently up into His eyes? Now look at the expression of love and admiration on Jesus' face. We know what He was thinking: "She is the only one in the room who understands I am going to die. I have told these disciples for at least the last year I would be going to Jerusalem to die, and they still don't get it. Mary is anointing my body with perfume for burial while I'm still alive and can enjoy it!"

Personally, I decided long ago I would rather have one rose I could smell and enjoy right now than ten thousand after I am dead and gone. I imagine you're like that, too.

Judas snarled, "Lord, tell her to stop! She is wasting that perfume!" Can we ever begin to feel and experience the pain caused by a betrayer? The Gospels tell us at that point the other disciples joined in criticizing her.

I used to think Jesus spoke the next sentence out of frustration and anger. But now, I think not. I believe He was filled with sorrow as He said, "Oh, Judas. Did you have to spoil it? I was really appreciating this moment. Mary is the only one who has figured out what's going on. She is anointing my body for burial. What she has done will be spoken as a memorial to her until I come again."

"What a waste!" Can you feel His pain?

Thursday night in the upper room, Jesus was sharing His last words with the disciples. He comforted them: *"Do not let your hearts be troubled. You believe in God; believe also in me. . . . And if I go and prepare a place for you, I will come back and take you to be with me that you also may be where I am. You know the way to the place where I am going." John 14:1-4 (NIV)*

Thomas replied, "Lord, we don't know where you're going, and we don't know how to get there." Imagine how much that hurt. Philip spoke up, "Yeah, we don't even know who you are!"

Can you believe that! He was making His final handoff before the cross, and they're fumbling the ball on the goal line. "Philip, have you been so long with me, and you still don't know who I am? Let's get this straight," he pleaded, "If you've seen me, you've seen the Father!"

He's on the way to the cross, not certain whether they even understood the basics.

Not long afterward He picked up the bread, blessed it, and passed it to His disciples: "This is my body which is broken for you. Take and eat." Then He took the chalice of wine and blessed it and passed it to His disciples: "This is my blood of the new covenant. Drink all of it."

Do you know what is the very next verse? Luke tells us: *"A dispute also arose among them as to which of them was considered to be the greatest." Luke 22:24 (NIV)* Can you imagine? Jesus is giving away his life for the sins of the world and they're arguing about which of them was the greatest! You know that hurt.

Later in the Garden of Gethsemane, Jesus said: *"My soul is overwhelmed with sorrow to the point of death. Stay here and keep watch with me." Matthew 26:38 (NIV)*

Did you just read those words? Or did you stop to consider *how* He said what He said? He was getting ready to die. He was mourning and grieving. Now do you hear the agony and pain?

He returned an hour later to find all of them asleep. He said to Peter, James, and John, "Could you not pray with me for one hour?" These are the words of a hurting Savior. Do you hear the sad disappointment? He wanted His disciples to put their arms around Him and comfort Him. But they were sound asleep.

He left to pray for another hour. This time the intensity was so powerful that the capillaries in His forehead burst, and he sweated drops of blood. He pleaded: "Father, is there any other way we can do this?" No, there was not. God sent angels to minister to Him.

By the way, God's primary design is for the people around us to comfort us when we hurt. When no one else is around, thank God for the angels.

Jesus returned to discover the disciples were sleeping again: "Wake up! The betrayer is at hand." Sure enough, Judas was guiding the band of soldiers to arrest Him. The betrayer walked directly to Jesus and kissed Him. This was no ordinary kiss. The Greek word used is the one reserved for a passionate lover's kiss. Listen to the next line: "Must you betray me with a passionate lover's kiss?" Do you hear the humiliation in His voice?

Shortly thereafter the trials, mocking, questionings, beatings, and crown of thorns commenced. Jesus held His hands still as the nails penetrated His flesh. Can you imagine the sorrow of being put to death by the very men you've created? Imagine the feelings of rejection: *"He came to that which was His own, but His own did not receive Him." John 1:11 (NIV)*

Then, the cross slammed into place.

He looked down to see the soldiers gambling for His robe and prayed, *"Father, forgive them, for they do not know what they are doing." Luke 23:34 (NIV)*

He saw His mother and the disciple whom He loved standing at the foot of His cross: "Woman, behold your son," He said to Mary. Then He said to John, "Behold your mother." Do you realize what just happened? It was Jesus' job to take care of Mary in her old age, and He was not going to be there. He was passing off the care of His mother to John. Don't think for a moment this didn't hurt?

Darkness covered the earth: "My God, my God, why have You forsaken me?"

"I thirst."

"It is finished. . . . Into Your hands I commit my spirit."

I am not sure we are ready to help hurting people with godly compassion until we can enter into the sufferings of Jesus.

Dear Lord Jesus,

May I join you in your pain and suffering on the cross? It is never good to grieve alone. My heart aches for you as you see the pain and suffering in your world. I know you will one day retake the world from the clutches of Satan, but that time has not yet come. Until it does, I want to feel your pains and grieve your hurts in order that I may bring f comfort to you. I pray for you to find peace and grace as you comfort and care for your children. I want to know better how I can bless your heart.

Please continue growing me to be a spiritual mother or father at any price.

Amen.

CHAPTER 6

LOOKING LIKE JESUS

God's primary purpose behind spiritual growth is to mold His children to look like Jesus.

His Outward Appearance

> Then God said, "Let us make man in our image" Genesis 1:26 (NIV)

Just for fun, let's consider what Jesus might have looked like when He was in His earthly body. Early in the third century A.D. "The Letter of Lentulus"[21] gave the only known physical description of Jesus. Holman Hunt used this description for his famous painting of Jesus folding His hands calmly in prayer.

> *There has appeared here in our time and still lives here, a man of great power named Jesus Christ. The people call him a prophet of truth, and his disciples, the Son of God. He has a venerable face, of a sort to arouse both fear and love in those who see him. His hair is the color of ripe chestnuts, smooth almost to the ears, but above them waving and curling, with a slight bluish radiance, and it flows over his shoulders. It is parted in the middle on the top of his head, after the fashion of the people of Nazareth. His brow is smooth and very calm, with a face without wrinkle or blemish, lightly tinged with red. His nose and mouth are faultless. His beard is luxuriant and unclipped, of the same color as his hair, not long but parted at the chin. His eyes are expressive and brilliant. His face is*

terrible in reproof, sweet and gentle in admonition, cheerful without ceasing to be grave. He has never been seen to laugh, but often to weep. His figure is slender and erect; his hands and arms are beautiful to see. His conversation is serious, sparing and modest. He is the fairest of the children of men.[21]

Some believe this portrayal to be nothing less than the police description of Jesus at the time of His arrest. "The Letter of Lentulus" is obviously a forgery—although it's possible it embodies to some degree a genuine picture passed down from the second century. It may be that we have to say with Augustine regarding the true physical appearance of Jesus, we are utterly ignorant.

Some look to Isaiah 53 and declare that Jesus was ugly. But remember this is a prophecy about what Jesus looked like as he was hanging on the cross.

> *He grew up before him like a tender shoot, and like a root out of dry ground.*
>
> *He had no beauty or majesty to attract us to him, nothing in his appearance that we should desire him.*
>
> *He was despised and rejected by mankind, a man of suffering, and familiar with pain.*
>
> *Like one from whom people hide their faces he was despised, and we held him in low esteem.*
>
> *Surely he took up our pain and bore our suffering,*
>
> *Yet we considered him punished by God, stricken by him, and afflicted.*
>
> *But he was pierced for our transgressions, he was crushed for our iniquities;*
>
> *the punishment that brought us peace was on him,*
>
> *And by his wounds we are healed.*
>
> *Isaiah 53:2-5 (NIV)*

On the other hand, Psalm 22—the Psalm of the Cross— describes what Jesus would see when He looked down from the cross.

My God, my God, why have you forsaken me? . . .
All who see me mock me;
they hurl insults, shaking their heads.
"He trusts in the Lord," they say,
"let the Lord rescue him.
Let him deliver him,
since he delights in him.". . .
Many bulls surround me;
strong bulls of Bashan encircle me.
Roaring lions that tear their prey
open their mouths wide against me.
I am poured out like water,
and all my bones are out of joint.
My heart has turned to wax;
it has melted within me.
My mouth is dried up like a potsherd,
and my tongue sticks to the roof of my mouth;
you lay me in the dust of death.
Dogs surround me,
a pack of villains encircles me;
they pierce my hands and my feet.
All my bones are on display;
people stare and gloat over me.
They divide my clothes among them
and cast lots for my garment. . . .
Posterity will serve him;
future generations will be told about the Lord.
They will proclaim his righteousness,
declaring to a people yet unborn:
He has done it!
Psalm 22 (NIV)

His Inner Character

In Matthew 11:29, we find the only time Jesus ever described an aspect of His inner character. Jesus said:

"Take my yoke upon you and learn from me, for I am gentle and humble in heart."

Looking like Jesus means developing an inner attitude of gentleness and humility. Paul used the Lord Jesus Christ as his model for the fruit of the Spirit recorded in Galatians:

"Love, joy, peace, forbearance, kindness, goodness, faithfulness, gentleness and self-control." Galatians 5:22-23 (NIV)

He also used Jesus as his model when he amplified the essence of love in 1 Corinthians 13:

Love is patient ... kind ... does not envy ... does not boast ... is not proud ... does not dishonor others ... is not self-seeking ... is not easily angered ... keeps no record of wrongs ... does not delight in evil but rejoices with the truth ... always protects ... always trusts ... always hopes ... always perseveres. Love never fails. 1 Corinthians 13:4-8 (NIV)

As we mature into spiritual mothers and fathers, we see not only the fruit of the spirit developing within us, we see the essence of love blossoming within us.

The Princess

You meet all sorts of fascinating people when traveling in Europe. Julie, Bronwyn, and I were in a cramped passenger train traveling from France to Switzerland. The rather intimidating British English professor sharing a compartment with us mentioned his two daughters were studying at Oxford. One was soon to be graduated as a lawyer and the other was finishing up her studies to enter medical school.

"What are you going to major in?" he asked our 14-year-old daughter.

"I guess I am still undecided."

"Well, is there anything you wanted to be when you grow up?"

Bronwyn paused a moment and then said, "A princess."

I imagine most girls dream of being Cinderella sometime during their growing up years.

As Christ followers we say: "I'm a Christian." As we mature spiritually our prayers reach upward to a higher level: "I want to grow up to look like Jesus at any price!" Christ doesn't come into our lives solely to forgive sins and give us a home in heaven. Christ enters our lives so He may put Himself on display for the entire world to see!

God's Good Purpose

Hopefully, early on in our spiritual growth we sort out the real meaning of Romans 8:28:

> *"And we know that in all things God works for the good of those who love him, who have been called according to his purpose." Romans 8:28 (NIV)*

We tend to focus on the "all things...work for good," and never move on to verse 29: "*For those God foreknew he also predestined to be conformed to the image of his Son..." Romans 8:29 (NIV)*

The "good" of verse 28 doesn't mean everything's going to turn out well. Things will not always turn out so well. It means all things work together for the good purpose of molding us to look like Jesus.

I once overheard a well-intentioned spiritual child say to a young woman who was struggling with cancer, "Don't worry, Valerie, God promised all things work together for good to those who love God, and we all know you love God, so be at peace. You are going to be fine!" Five months later I performed Valerie's funeral. All things did not work out the way the spiritual child promised.

Too many Christians imagine the "good" of Romans 8:28 stands alone. It doesn't. God didn't promise Valerie would recover from cancer. What He promised was that her experience with cancer would be allowed and designed by the Father for the *good purpose* of molding her will to look like Jesus.

Miles Stanford observed in Principles of Spiritual Growth:

> *The open secret of healthy spiritual growth is to know and settle upon this fact as set forth in Romans 8:28-29. When we*

see that all things are working together to make us more and more like the Lord Jesus, we will not be frustrated and upset when some of these "things" are hard, difficult to understand, and often contain an element of death. We will be able to rest in our Lord Jesus and say to our Father, "Thy will be done." And our constant attitude of faith will be: "Though he slay me, yet will I trust in him" (Job 13:15). This is our matriculation to spiritual maturity.[22]

The Image of God

Had anyone been in the Garden of Eden before the fall of Adam and Eve, he or she would see in Adam a reflection of God the Father because Adam was made in the image of God. Unfortunately, when we turn the page to Genesis 3:1-6, we discover Adam's and Eve's sin detonated an emotional, mental, physical, and spiritual bomb. In Genesis 5:1-3, Adam and Eve conceived a son named Seth who was born in man's image—not God's. One of the consequences of sin was that the image of God was no longer visible on earth.

When Jesus put on a body and became a man, the image of God was back on earth!

"In the past God spoke to our ancestors through the prophets at many times and in various ways, but in these last days he has spoken to us by his Son. . . the exact representation of his being." Hebrews 1:1-3 (NIV)

The image of God disappeared when wicked men crucified Christ. For three days, the image was hidden inside a tomb. At the resurrection, the image was once again on display. During the next 40 days, Jesus appeared to over 500 different individuals. However, as He ascended into the heavens, the image of God once more disappeared from view.

Now, here is where we come in! On Pentecost, ten days after the ascension, the Holy Spirit descended as living tongues of fire and settled on, and then indwelt, 120 believers (Acts 2:1-4). Once again, the image of God was back on earth—multiplied—in the lives of 120 new Christians.

In the upper room discourse (John 13-17), Jesus told His disciples it was good for Him to go away. They did not join in His enthusiasm because they failed to see the big picture. When Jesus was stilling the storm on the Sea of Galilee, He could not be in Jerusalem telling Nicodemus how he could be born again. In his earthly body He was limited to one place at one time.

Today, the image is visible, not just in one location, but in hundreds and thousands of places throughout the world—wherever there are followers of Jesus Christ. Now, through the lives of His followers, He is everywhere all the time.

> *"And we all, who with unveiled faces contemplate the Lord's glory, are being transformed into his image with ever-increasing glory, which comes from the Lord, who is the Spirit."*
> *2 Corinthians 3:18 (NIV)*

Space Trilogy

Growing to maturity takes a long time. One of the main reasons the transformation proceeds slowly is we have such little appreciation for the infinite distance between God and us.

One evening, Richard prayed in my living room, "Lord Jesus, please let us see ourselves from Your perspective." Too often we compare ourselves with others to see how we are doing in our spiritual lives. What might it do to our understanding if we could see ourselves from His perspective!

When I was ten years old, dad took me to the Braniff Airways Building in Dallas where he worked. As we walked along the sidewalk, he called my attention to the difference in people's heights. Some were five-feet tall; some six-feet-six-inches tall, and everything in between. Moments later, we were on the 10th floor balcony looking over the rail at the sidewalk far below. Dad said, "Now look at the people on the sidewalk. Can you tell the difference between the five-footers and six-and-one-half footers?"

"No, not from ten stories up! They all look the same!"

"Let this be a lesson to you." (He said that a lot.) "From our perspective people look good or bad and everything in between. But from God's perspective, people all look alike. None of us is close to God's level. A huge chasm exists between God and us."

That's one reason why we all need a Savior.

In his *Space Trilogy* (*Out of the Silent Planet*[23], *Perelandra*[24], and *That Hideous Strength*[25]), C. S. Lewis used science fiction to sort out the implications of mankind's stumbling fall into sin (Genesis 3). In the first volume, *Out of the Silent Planet*, Lewis pondered what Thulcandra (our earth) might be like if mankind and sin had not contaminated it.

Lewis imagined every planet in the universe was overseen by an angelic creature called an "Oyarsa." Once a year, the Oyarsas throughout the universe gathered for their annual convention. However, Lucifer, the Oyarsa who oversaw Earth, (Thulcandra) never attended. In fact, no communication ever emanated from Thulcandra. The Oyarsas knew something horrible had once occurred on Thulcandra and that God's creation there was "bent." The creatures there were so bent they couldn't even see angels!

We know what a "bent" race looks like. We are one! How far have we fallen? What might an original, pristine, pure, unbent world be like?

In *Out of the Silent Planet,* four races of sinless sentient beings (human-like—but not really human) lived on a planet named Malacandra. Lucifer escaped to Malacandra on a rocket ship constructed by Dr. Weston (Satan incarnate) and was engaged in seducing the four unfallen races of Malacandra to fall into sin. Providentially, Ransom, the novel's hero, is nearby. The name Ransom is both his name and a play on words describing Jesus as being the ransom for our sins. Weston and his partner intended to use Ransom as a sacrifice.

Perelandra is the name of both the second book in the trilogy and the water-covered planet with only two inhabitants, neither of whom has sinned. After returning to earth, Dr. Weston journeyed to Perelandra with a mission to seduce those two into sin. The Queen and the Lady Mother face the choice between obedience to God or following the path of the "bent," Silent Planet.

We live in a world where the choice to sin or not is already made. We have no clue as to what an un-fallen world might be like. Fortunately, God planned for our restoration. Peter described this restoration concept of the indwelling Christ:

> *"... you may participate in the divine nature, having escaped the corruption in the world caused by evil desires." 2 Peter 1:4 (NIV)*

Paul explained it like this:

"To them God has chosen to make known among the Gentiles the glorious riches of this mystery, which is Christ in you, the hope of glory." Colossians 1:27 (NIV)

Failure at Grandy's

Before Christ's indwelling, our human spirits are in a coma-like state. At the moment of salvation, the Holy Spirit accomplishes what the Bible refers to as His regenerating work of renewal (Titus 3:5). He turns on the light in our innermost human spirit so we become spiritually alive and positively inclined toward spiritual things (1 Corinthians 2:11-15).

Unfortunately, at any time we can behave in such way that we fail to look much like Jesus. I was standing in line with Julie, Bronwyn, and Brie at Grandy's fast-food restaurant, waiting for our turn to order. We knew exactly what we wanted. We eat lunch there often. I was tired after preaching four sermons that morning. All I wanted was a quick lunch and to go home to bed for a nap.

The two college girls who were standing in front of us were looking at the menu and obviously unable to decide what to order. I was more than a little impatient. Finally, not able to stand it any longer, I stepped in front of the young ladies and said to the woman behind the counter, "Well, if they aren't ready, we are. We want four family meals ..."

One of the college girls grinned at me, stuck out her hand, and said, "Hi, my name is Jill and this is my friend Amanda. We're students at the University of Arizona and we wanted to tell you how much we enjoyed your sermon this morning!"

Driving home in the car, Julie said, "You didn't look a lot like Jesus, did you?" No, I came off looking like a spiritual five-year-old. I'll have to practice my manners if I want to look more like Jesus.

How Much Like Jesus

By the way, how much do you look like Jesus? What do people think of when they think of you? Perhaps they think "she's a saleswoman," or "he's an accountant." Perhaps they observe "she has nine children." Maybe the first thing they think of is your political persuasion or your marital state. But wouldn't it be nice when your name comes up in conversation people's first thoughts about you were "she reminds me a lot of Jesus," or "he's a spiritual man," or "she's a godly woman!"

Some people are so deeply associated with one thing or another that when we think of them, we naturally think of that thing or event. What is the first thing you think of when you hear the name Billy Graham? You think "worldwide evangelist." Bill Gates? Computers! Alexander Graham Bell? Telephone.

When your name comes up in conversation, what do people think?

Wouldn't it be nice if you reminded them of Jesus?

Charles Spurgeon pastored in London during the latter half of the 19th century. Eighteen thousand copies of his sermons were printed and distributed worldwide each week. He was one of the greatest preachers this world has known.

Joseph Parker also preached in London during the same period. He, too, was famous the world over. After hearing Parker preach, the most often heard comment as people departed the People's Church was, "Joseph Parker is a wonderful preacher."

Many of those same folks went later that afternoon to hear Spurgeon preach. The most frequently heard comment as people departed Spurgeon's Metropolitan Tabernacle was, "Oh! That Jesus! What a wonderful Savior."

Do you see the difference? God is not interested in putting us on display. He's concerned with putting Jesus Christ is on display.

> *"But we have this treasure in jars of clay to show that this all-surpassing power is from God and not from us. We are hard pressed on every side, but not crushed; perplexed, but not in despair; persecuted, but not abandoned; struck down, but not destroyed. We always carry around in our body the death of Jesus, so that the life of Jesus may also be revealed in our body." 2 Corinthians 4:7-10 (NIV)*

Dear Father,

Use whatever tools necessary to mold me into the image of Christ.

Amen.

CHAPTER 7

GOD'S TOOLBOX

Brokenness puts Christ on display.

The Christmas season was under way. I was concluding a three-month class on the basic principles of spiritual growth. "Are there any final questions?" I asked.

An obviously pregnant woman raised her hand and said, "You may have noticed I've not said anything since I began coming to this class. I attend another church. But I heard about this class and wanted to come. I've wanted to ask a question but was too shy. However, I really want to know … if I begin to pray to be a spiritual mother at any price, is there a chance God might take my baby?"

"I wish I had dismissed the class ten minutes earlier!" I joked. Everyone chuckled nervously. "The truth is, I can think of some extreme scenarios where your question might come into play. However, I certainly wouldn't worry about it. You go ahead and pray for God to make you a spiritual mother at any price. I'm sure your baby will be fine."

I was working in my office several days after the New Year when my phone rang: "Hi. I'm the pregnant woman in your spiritual growth class who asked if God might take my baby if I began to pray to be a spiritual woman at any price. Remember me?"

"Yes, of course, I remember you."

"I went home that night and began to pray to be a spiritual mother at any price. I just wanted you to know that I gave birth to my baby three days ago. My baby lived for six hours. I just returned home from the funeral. Could you come over and see me?"

I was stunned—and felt awful.

What should I say? What should I not say? Would it do any good to try to explain? Explain what? Should I just keep my mouth shut and let her do all the talking? Oh, God, help me!

I parked and walked up the sidewalk. When her husband opened the door, I saw her resting in a recliner. Her husband invited me to sit on the couch. She spoke first, "I wanted you to know that I may never know if there was any connection between my prayer to be a spiritual mother and the death of my baby. But I do know this—God will use even this for the good purpose of molding me to look like Jesus. Thank you."

In this case, He used the tools of discipleship and sanctification to accomplish his crucifying work.

Come and Die

In *The Cost of Discipleship*[26] Dietrich Bonhoeffer declared: "When Jesus Christ calls a man, He bids him come and die." While circumstances vary from person to person, the process remains the same for all.

God utilizes a tool we call brokenness to allow the internal Christ to be put on outward display. In John 12:24, Jesus picked up a little seed, held it in His hand, and said to His disciples:

"Very truly I tell you, unless a kernel of wheat falls to the ground and dies, it remains only a single seed. But if it dies, it produces many seeds." (NIV)

The issue is not, is there life in the seed? There's life in the seed. The question is, has the shell broken for the life to come forth?

The question for Christians is not, is there divine life inside the Christian? Divine life lives inside of the Christian. The question is, has the shell broken for the resurrected Christ to come out?

When we were in high school my brother Ronnie and I raced pigeons. After a time, we began raising fancy pigeons: fantails, rollers, muff-tumblers, and just common, everyday pigeons. We named them all and flew them all. We nailed apple crates to the insides of our coop for nests, put in straw, and the birds would mate. Soon, little eggs filled the nests. We were so excited.

One morning broken shells were all over the nests! We didn't mind. Under momma pigeons, cute, tiny, featherless little squabs were cooing for breakfast. Eggs are nice, but baby pigeons are nicer!

God intends to break through our outside shells so people may see the Lord Jesus Christ who lives within us, and for the Lord Jesus within us to be free to come forth and minister to people around us.

In the following diagram, the two circles represent two individuals. One is a new Christian—recently indwelt by Jesus Christ. The other person is not yet a Christian.

The circles represent our outside selves, our personalities, wishes, wants, and desires—what people know about us when they see and interact with us.

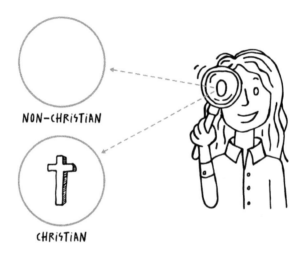

NON-CHRISTIAN

CHRISTIAN

To most observers, spiritual children and non-Christians look startlingly alike. The lack of spiritual growth explains why many new Christians (and spiritual children who refuse to grow up) are called hypocrites. They still look and act much like they did before they met Christ.

However, there is a vast difference between spiritual children and non-Christians. Christ has not yet had time to make the inner transformations that will one day manifest in Christ-like behaviors.

Metaphorically speaking, God has a wide selection of hammers and wedges to use in sculpting us to look like Jesus. They may include challenging trials, painful life events, failed relationships, and serious illnesses. When He decides to process a part of our lives that needs attention, He selects a small hammer and a small wedge and begins to hit carefully on just the right spot.

GOD'S TOOL BOX

SMALL HAMMER
(FOR LIGHT
SPIRITUAL NUTURING)

When God begins to hammer, the normal response is "God, why me? Why is it *my* baby who died? Why did we have the car wreck? Why did my business go down the drain?"

Instead of submitting to God and thanking Him for using a particular trial or trouble to make us more like Jesus, we tend to get bitter and angry. We get hard and calloused at the very point where He intends to work. So, our God says, "No problem. I can handle that." He just gets a bigger wedge and a bigger hammer!

GOD'S TOOL BOX

MASSIVE HAMMER
(FOR A BIG
REMODELING JOB)

How do you react in the face of problems? How do you respond when tragedy occurs? Do you get angry and bitter? Do you give up in despair? Do you quietly submit to God's hand at work in your life?

Of course, troubles and difficulties are not the only tools God uses. He utilizes numerous less painful tools like discipleship, Bible study, fellowship, and prayer just to name a few.

Now is the time to rest on the promise that all things work together for the good purpose of making us look like Jesus Christ.

Adopting this outlook is the only way to fulfill Paul's dream that we rejoice at all times in the midst of all circumstances. When we accept the principle of brokenness, we more easily engage with Romans 5:3-5:

> *"More than that, we rejoice in our sufferings, knowing that suffering produces endurance, and endurance produces character, and character produces hope, and hope does not disappoint us, because God's love has been poured into our hearts through the Holy Spirit which has been given to us." (RSV)*

Understanding the concept of brokenness makes it easier for us to enter into the experience of Ephesians 5:20: "*... always giving thanks to God the Father for everything, in the name of our Lord Jesus Christ.*" (NIV)

Paul continued this theme in 1 Thessalonians 5:16-18: "*Rejoice always; pray continually; give thanks in all circumstances, for this is God's will for you in Christ Jesus.*" (NIV)

Second Choice

Very few Christians live out their lives based on their first choice. One test of maturity is how we handle second best. We can thank God for our troubles and rejoice during them only when we can say with deep confidence, "Thank You, God. I understand that even this difficult time in my life is allowed by you for the good purpose of making me look like Jesus."

The shell of spiritual children is still mostly intact. God's breaking work is showing results; but frankly, spiritual children don't yet look much like Jesus. There are but a few places where Jesus can minister freely through a spiritual child—and there aren't many places for others to see through the child's self-reliance, self-centeredness, and self-condemnation to observe the Jesus who lives within.

Spiritual young men and women have substantial gaps in their shells where God is accomplishing His breaking work. Brokenness is progressing well.

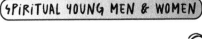

Hardly any shell remains visible around spiritual mothers and fathers. People can see vast amounts of Christ within them and His ability to work out through them is greatly enhanced.

The preceding circles are descriptive models of what it means for a little grain of wheat to fall in the ground and die. As the shell breaks, more and more of the life emerges.

Consider this insight from Miles Stanford in *Principles of Spiritual Growth*:

> *"It is one thing to know what God's purpose is for our lives, and it is another to know something of the 'how' as to entering into it all right here and now. One of God's most effective means in the process is failure. Many believers are simply frantic over the fact of failure in their lives, and they will go to all lengths in trying to hide it, ignore it, or rationalize about it. And all the time they are resisting the main instrument in the Father's hand for conforming us to the image of His Son!*
>
> *"Failure where self is concerned in our Christian life and service is allowed and often engineered by God in order to turn us completely from ourselves to His source for our life—Jesus Christ, who never fails"* [28]

Even Jesus needed to grow to spiritual maturity: *"And the child grew and became strong; he was filled with wisdom, and the grace of God was on him." Luke 2:40 (NIV)*

"Son though he was, he learned obedience from what he suffered, and once made perfect, he became the source of eternal salvation for all who obey him." Hebrews 5:8-9 (NIV)

Too many young Christians want an easy Christianity. But I see nothing easy here. I do see a tremendous plan and a great purpose.

In Hebrews 12:5-8, the writer got personal:

> And have you completely forgotten this word of encouragement that addresses you as a father addresses his son? It says,
>
> *"My son, do not make light of the Lord's discipline,*
>
>   *and do not lose heart when he rebukes you,*
>
> *because the Lord disciplines the one he loves,*
>
>   *and he chastens everyone he accepts as his son."*
>
> Endure hardship as discipline; God is treating you as his children. For what children are not disciplined by their

father? If you are not disciplined—and everyone undergoes discipline—then you are not legitimate, not true sons and daughters at all. (NIV)

Notice the relationship here: "The Lord disciplines the one he loves." Have you ever seen some child giving his mother fits in the grocery store? You come around the corner and he's pulling cereal boxes off the shelves, and you want to say something like, "Stop it! Behave! Straighten up!" But you never do that. Why? He's not your child. You don't discipline someone else's children.

From a love context, Jesus says, "I want you to be somebody special."

I carefully disciplined my children when they misbehaved. I tried to discipline with a heart of love: "I love you too much to let you get away with that sort of behavior. Mom and I want you to be someone special." Then, I proceeded with appropriate discipline. If we try to discipline a child to whom we have not shown much love, we will mess up the relationship every single time!

In Hebrews 12:9-11, the writer shared the reason for God's disciplining hand:

Moreover, we have all had human fathers who disciplined us and we respected them for it. How much more should we submit to the Father of spirits and live! They disciplined us for a little while as they thought best; but God disciplines us for our good, in order that we may share in his holiness. No discipline seems pleasant at the time, but painful. Later on, however, it produces a harvest of righteousness and peace for those who have been trained by it. (NIV)

According to the writer to the Hebrews, several improper responses can occur when a tragedy comes, or suffering arises, or a trial presents itself. He says: Don't allow a root of bitterness into your life. Don't make light of God's disciplining work. Don't lose hope and quit on Christ when the going gets tough. When God has His hand on your life, don't slough it off.

When God uses His hammers and wedges, the proper response is to "submit to the Father of spirits and live." Submitting might look something like this: "Thank You, God. I understand this trouble, this trial, this tragedy is designed and allowed by you for the purpose of sculpting me to look like Jesus."

The Perfume Bottle

The principle of brokenness runs relentlessly through the pages of Scripture from Genesis to Revelation. Chronologically, Job was the first Bible book written and the idea of brokenness was implanted early in Scripture. During his trials, Job cried out: *"But he knows the way that I take; when he has tried me, I shall come forth as gold."* *Job 23:10 (NIV)*

Joseph was processed as a slave and prisoner in Egypt. Moses learned the victory belonged to God in frightening encounters with Pharaoh. Jeremiah matured in a cistern in Israel. God asked Hosea to marry a prostitute.

Once upon a time, while Jesus was in Bethany having dinner in the home of Simon the Leper, a woman came with an alabaster jar of extremely expensive perfume. She broke open the jar and poured the perfume all over Jesus' head (see Mark 14:3). She was anointing his body for burial. Expensive perfume cascaded down over his head and onto His feet.

We are forever indebted to Judas for totaling up the value of the perfume. He figured she was pouring out about one year's wages on Jesus! It's as if Judas is saying, "Lord, tell her to stop! She's wasting it all on you!

Many speculate this perfume was Mary's life savings, her retirement fund. True or not, we do not know, but this is true: she poured out the very best she had on Jesus!

This entire experience is a metaphor. Like the seed in John 12:24, the real issue in the Christian life is not: Is there perfume (the Lord Jesus) inside the bottle (our bodies)? The real question is: Has the bottle been broken so the perfume can come out?

Many Christians love their perfume bottle more than they love Jesus. They will go to the utmost extreme to keep their little perfume bottles intact. We dare not hold back. Breaking the perfume bottle is the processing of the cross. We pour it all out on Jesus.

2 Corinthians 4:7 says, *"We have this treasure in jars of clay."* *(NIV)* The jars of clay are our human bodies. We are made out of dust and clay. The "treasure" is God Himself. Think of the miracle! We have this treasure, God Himself, dwelling in our jars of clay!

The divine nature is inside of us. Why? Paul continued: *"... to show that this all-surpassing power is from God and not from us."* God is not interested in whether people are impressed with us. He's not interested in showing off our abilities and talents. He is desperately concerned, however, with showing off Jesus.

Paul wrote:

> *"We are hard-pressed on every side, but not crushed; perplexed, but not in despair; persecuted, but not abandoned; struck down, but not destroyed. We always carry around in our body the death of Jesus, so that the life of Jesus may also be revealed in our body. For we who are alive are always being given over to death for Jesus' sake, so that his life may be revealed in our mortal body"* 2 Corinthians 4:8-11 (NIV)

When difficulties come, the spiritually immature may say, "God, why me? I didn't know good Christians would have troubles like mine!"

On the other hand, mature Christians say something like this: "Oh God, this hurts. But, I understand what is going on. Like Paul, I rejoice that you are using this difficulty to make me look more like Jesus. Thank You, God. I wouldn't miss out on this for the world!"

I've often thought I would never have chosen to endure heart surgery when I was 13—especially when nothing was wrong with my heart. On the other hand, as I think about it now, I wouldn't have missed those maturing lessons for anything in the world.

Our goal is the resurrected life of Jesus Christ—not the suffering of the process. The cross is the means to the resurrection, not the result.

When I teach my spiritual growth classes, two issues dominate the question-and-answer period after this lesson. One has to do with fear. The other has to do with anger.

Many react with a sense of fear. One woman was close to tears as she said, "I am afraid. I am a mother. I have children. I want to pray this prayer for God to make me a spiritual mother at any price, but I'm afraid something bad will happen to me or my children."

I hope that my answer now is a little better than the one I gave to the pregnant woman at the end of my class that Christmas season.

I responded, "Be at peace. Praying this prayer may sound scary, but the Bible tells us the Lord does not give us a spirit of fear."

In fact, the Bible tells us that as we experience God's love, His perfect love drives out fear (see 1 John 4:18). The more intimately we know God's heart, the more we experience His overwhelming love. His ultimate goal is for our good.

> *Which of you, if your son asks for bread, will give him a stone? Or if he asks for a fish, will give him a snake? If you, then, though you are evil, knowhow to give good gifts to your children, how much more will your Father in heaven give good gifts to those who ask him! Matthew 7:9-11 (NIV)*

Another common response is anger. When I was a child, my mother taught me a loving God would never send any kind of pain or suffering to His children. She was wrong. At the close of this lesson, many of my students—especially spiritual children—don't like the idea that a loving God might send difficulties to His children.

"I am angry to think God would send troubles to his children. That doesn't seem very loving. I am angry you said that!"

But remember, we don't base our theology on the opinions, feelings or musings of what people think ought to be right. We get our theology from the Bible. The Bible says God has no hesitation about allowing trouble to come to His people at the right times and for the right reasons.

The Old Testament prophet Habakkuk struggled deeply when God told him He intended to send the wicked, pagan Babylonians to make war on Israel because of Israel's sin of spiritual adultery. Habakkuk was angry with God: "You mean you're going to use the bad guys to inflict punishment on your people, the good guys? That isn't right!"

God responded, "Yes! That is exactly what I'm going to do." Five times Habakkuk questioned God about things he didn't understand. Each time God gave an answer that infuriated and confused Habakkuk even more. Yet, in the end, Habakkuk surrendered to God's plan and then pronounced one of the greatest statements of faith in all of Scripture:

> *Though the fig tree does not bud,*
> *and there are no grapes on the vines,*
> *Though the olive crop fails,*

and the fields produce no food,

Though there are no sheep in the pen,

and no cattle in the stalls,

yet I will rejoice in the Lord,

I will be joyful in God my Savior.

Habakkuk 3:17-18 (NIV)

Don't be afraid and don't be angry. Nothing comes to us except that which is allowed and designed by God for the very good purpose of sculpting us to look like Jesus.

"Many strive, few attain," is a long-believed, well-tested spiritual growth principle. There are a few, not many, but a few who say, "God, I want to be a spiritual woman or man. I don't care what it costs." God promises to answer that prayer.

Dear Jesus,

Would you please develop within me a heart to become a spiritual mother or father at any price?

Amen

CHAPTER 8

CROSS TRAINING

Jesus died for us on the cross of salvation. We die with Jesus on the cross of sanctification.

A resolution was presented at the annual meeting of the Southern Baptist Convention in Houston, Texas. I will paraphrase: "I move that we purchase a 30-second commercial spot during the next Super Bowl, condense the gospel into 30 seconds and we can share the gospel with 100 million people at one time!" The applause was thunderous!

That evening, Chuck Colson addressed the meeting on the subject of cheap versus costly grace. He based his talk on the book by Dietrich Bonhoeffer, *The Cost of Discipleship*. Bonhoeffer distinguishes between cheap grace, which doesn't us cost anything, and costly grace, which will cost us our lives. Bonhoeffer summarized costly grace like this: "When Jesus Christ calls a man, He bids him come and die."[29]

Chuck Colson then said, "We have lost the New Testament concept of the value of grace. No longer are we preaching the kind of gospel which confronts men and women with the demand for their entire lives. We are offering cheap grace instead of costly grace! It won't surprise me if we soon start selling Jesus Christ like we sell soap!"

A hush fell over the group. Immediately, I thought that certainly he had missed the morning session. Then I realized he hadn't.

Jesus said to his disciples in Luke 9:23-25:

Whoever wants to be my disciple must deny themselves and take up their cross daily and follow me. For whoever wants to save their life will lose it, but whoever loses their life for me will save it. What good is it for someone to gain the whole world, and yet lose or forfeit their very self? (NIV)

In this chapter I want to discuss with you what dying on a cross look like. Where did Jesus take His cross? To Golgotha. What did He do with it? He died on it. Where do we take our cross? To Golgotha, and like Jesus, we die there. Jesus Christ is calling us to get into the electric chair! Jesus Christ is calling us to give away our lives and follow him at any price.

Two Crosses

Two crosses loom before us as we continue our spiritual journey. One is at the narrow, confining door of salvation. On this cross, Jesus died in order to forgive our sins and make us fit for heaven. However, the work of the cross is not finished at conversion. The cross of sanctification is God's primary tool whereby Christ's makes us fit to live on earth.

> *"I have been crucified with Christ and I no longer live, but Christ lives in me. The life I live in the body I live by faith in the Son of God, who loved me and gave himself for me." Galatians 2:20 (NIV)*

A. W. Tozer made a sweeping declaration about the cost of following Jesus:

It is doubtful that God has ever used a man or woman greatly until He has first hurt him or her deeply.

I want to detail three things about dying on a cross and how each applies to our spiritual processing: (1) Dying on a cross hurts. (2) Dying on a cross takes time. (3) Self-crucifixion is impossible.

1. Dying on a cross hurts.

Crucifixion is a cruel way to die. Scourgings and beatings produce blood loss and dehydration. Inserting nails at carefully calculated angles by bending the ankles sideways against a vertical wood piece, then hammering nails through the ankles, produces excruciating pain. The body is in shock. A ruptured heart often brings on a cataclysmic death.

Scientists are now able to measure the intensity of pain. A migraine hurts more than a skinned knee. They have determined that two of the most painful things human beings can experience are giving birth and passing a kidney stone.

But the two are so different. Passing a kidney stone is simply pointless suffering. On the other hand, the pains of childbirth have meaning. This is why the person who passes a kidney stone will say, "I never want to go through that again." However, the mother who gives birth may eventually say, "Honey, I think I am ready to have another baby."

No one wants to suffer for nothing (a kidney stone). We handle it better if we are suffering for something (a baby). In terms of spiritual growth, our sufferings are not wasted. They are for Jesus!

Peter spoke of the painful cross of sanctification in graphic detail:

> *In all this you greatly rejoice, though now for a little while you may have had to suffer grief in all kinds of trials. These have come so that the proven genuineness of your faith—of greater worth than gold, which perishes even though refined by fire—may result in praise, glory and honor when Jesus Christ is revealed. 1 Peter 1:6-7 (NIV)*

Peter compares the purifying of faith to the process of refining gold. The goldsmith puts gold ore in a crucible, lights a fire beneath it and watches the ore melt. Since gold is a very heavy metal, it sinks to the bottom of the crucible while impurities rise to the top. As the process continues, the goldsmith systematically skims off the impurities. When he can see his face perfectly reflected inside the crucible, he knows the gold is pure.

In the same way, there are times when God puts us in the crucible and turns up the heat. He skims off our impurities as they rise to the top, leaving only the gold of a purified life. Jesus knows His work is finished when He sees his face perfectly reflected in our lives.

God has placed a thermometer inside every crucible which is calibrated with the letters "L-O-V-E." He monitors the flame and the temperature, making it just hot enough, for just long enough, to boil away our impurities. Remember:

No temptation has overtaken you except what is common to mankind. And God is faithful; he will not let you be tempted beyond what you can bear. But when you are tempted, he will also provide a way out so that you can endure it." 1 Corinthians 10:13 (NIV)

Do you know how they temper steel? It is beaten and molded into just the right shape. Then it's heated until it's white-hot. Then it's quickly immersed into a vat of ice-cold brine—and the steel screams. When it's withdrawn it's tempered. Molecules are realigned during the heating and the quick cooling process that produces tremendous strength.

Dr. Harry Ironside was a masterful Bible expositor. He wrote a commentary on almost every book in the Bible. One of his students came to him with a request: "Dr. Ironside, I'm having difficulty with patience. Would you please pray God would give me patience?"

"Certainly."

They got on their knees and Dr. Ironside prayed, "Dear Father, would you please send this young brother some problems?"

Knowing that Ironside was hard of hearing, the student interrupted Ironsides' prayer: "Hold it, Dr. Ironside, no, no, no. I don't want problems. I want patience."

Ironside said, "Then, let's pray again." They bowed their heads: "Dear Father, please send this young man some problems."

"No, no, no, no. I don't want problems. I want patience."

Dr. Ironside quoted James 1:2-4:

Consider it pure joy, my brothers and sisters, whenever you face trials of many kinds, because you know that the testing of your faith develops perseverance. Let perseverance finish its work so that you may be mature and complete, not lacking anything. (NIV)

Ironside then continued, "Troubles and problems are what produce the patience you so desire."

Not long after our conversion God maneuvers us face-to-face with the cross of sanctification. It sits in a giant, seemingly uncrossable abyss. The only way to cross to the resurrection side of spiritual mother and fatherhood is by dying on the cross of sanctification.

Standing at the edge of this spiritual precipice we decide whether to proceed or slide back to spiritual childhood. There is no third option.

At this point, most Christians turn around and head back toward the door of salvation, choosing to remain baby Christians. However, a few—not many, but a few—are willing to suffer on the cross of sanctification.

The cross is not an end unto itself. Remember, no one can have a resurrection until they first have a cross. We are striving for resurrection life and power.

As we commit to the process of maturity, God replies, " I will put you on the cross." So, he often places that child on the cross—in the midst of the crucible, and He turns up the heat.

Our initial response to the process is, "God, what's going on here?"

God replies, "Don't you understand? I'm answering your prayer."

"But I want to be like Jesus."

"Well, this is how I do it."

Elijah

The processing of Elijah is a classic example of how God uses the sanctifying cross to sculpt a man or woman of God. 1 Kings 17:1 begins with the words, "Elijah the Tishbite." Tishbe was Elijah's hometown. The chapter concludes 24 verses later by describing Elijah as "the man of God." I want to know what occurred during those 24 verses that transformed Elijah from the nondescript "Tishbite" into "Elijah the man of God."

The chapter begins with Elijah praying for a drought. He announced to King Ahab that no rain or dew would fall until God directed otherwise. Immediately after the announcement, God instructed Elijah to go to the Kerith Ravine and hide himself.

Elijah lived the life of luxury by the Kerith Ravine. God instructed the ravens to bring him meat and potatoes and hot rolls and blueberry pie and iced tea. At least that's what my Sunday School teacher taught me when I was 10 years old.

As I got older, I realized ravens were the scavengers of the desert. What did they bring him to eat? Old dead cow carcasses and sheep remains. After all, cows and sheep were dying by the thousands in the drought. Fortunately, at least he had water, until the brook dried up. Then, Elijah complained: "God, what's going on here? The brook dried up."

God said, "What do you expect when you pray for no rain?" Please note the Hebrew word "Kerith" means "to cut, to peel, or to file."

Please don't despise the educational experience of a drying brook. Did God know the brook was going to dry up? Certainly. Was Elijah in the middle of God's will? Surely. However, the drying brook didn't seem like God's plan to the thirsty Elijah: "God, this couldn't be the plan. Something surely has gone wrong. Is this how You treat Your preachers? Where's my water?"

God replied firmly, "You're exactly where I want you."

Sooner or later, maturing Christians understand that drying brooks are God's crucibles for making men and women of God.

Abraham was growing in the faith when God said, "Sacrifice your boy." Right then, Abraham's brook dried up.

Joseph was his father's favorite son. Life was great until the day his brothers put him in a pit and his brook dried up.

Paul was on his first missionary journey, spreading the gospel, when he was stoned and left for dead in Lystra. His brook dried up.

Jesus said to his disciples in John 6, "Get inside the boat and go to the other side of the lake." That night, a seismographic storm arose and they were terrified. "What in the world are we doing out here in this storm?"

Jesus could've said it like this, "You are exactly where I want you to be."

From the parched brook, God sent Elijah to Zarephath. There was a smelter in Zarephath; and the town was named after the smelter. Zarephath means, "to melt." Ninety miles separated the Kerith Ravine from Zarephath—90 miles with no water. Remember the drought? Depending on the time of year, 90 miles without water is fatal. The cutting was done. Now, the melting began.

God told Elijah a widow would care for him when he arrived in Zarephath. In their culture for a man to be cared for by a woman was a most humiliating proposition.

In Zarephath, God melted Elijah. While he was in the care of the widow (to make a long story short), Elijah soon came under ridicule and accusation because of the sickness and subsequent death of the widow's son. Those who walk with God long enough will discover God's trials come back-to-backto-back. They certainly did for Elijah.

"Go to Kerith," God instructed him. "Let me cut and peel and break you. Go to Zarephath. I'm going to melt you."

The Shaping of a Disciple, by Dale Martin Stone, summarizes God's sanctifying work of the cross:

"When God wants to drill a man,

And thrill a man, and skill a man,

When God wants to mold a man

To play for Him the noblest part,

When He yearns with all His heart

To build so great and bold a man

That all the world shall be amazed,

Then watch God's methods, watch His ways!

How He ruthlessly perfects

Whom He royally elects;

How He hammers him and hurts him

And with mighty blows converts him,

Making shapes and forms which only

God Himself can understand,

Even while his man is crying,

Lifting a beseeching hand...

Yet God bends but never breaks

When man's good He undertakes;

When He uses whom He chooses,

And with every purpose fuses

Man to act, and act to man,

As it is when He began,

When God tries His splendor out,

Man will know what He's about![30]

Only after God shaped him at the Kerith Ravine and melted him at Zarephath was Elijah ready to call down fire on Mt. Carmel. He wasn't ready in chapter 16. He wasn't yet a man of God. Now, at the end of 1 Kings 17, he's molded and mature, and God said, "Now you're ready, Elijah. Let's go call down fire."

Of course, not every Christian is asked to call down fire on Mt. Carmel. What God does to prepare a person to call down fire, and the processing he needs to prepare someone to care for babies in the church nursery, are two entirely different things.

The people who make a tremendous difference in God's Kingdom on earth are not the young spiritual children huddling in fear by the door of salvation. The ones who make the most impact are those who stand on the mountain peaks as spiritual mothers and fathers.

2. Dying on a cross takes time.

The Roman historian Tacitus wrote that the longest he watched someone struggle on a cross was six days. Dying on a cross was a slow, agonizing process.

In terms of our spiritual growth, Jesus is not in a hurry. He's not working for tomorrow morning. He is working for eternity. Spiritual growth takes time.

> "Being confident of this, that he who began a good work in you will carry it on to completion until the day of Christ Jesus."
> Philippians 1:6 (NIV)

Moses declared in Psalm 90:4:

> "For a thousand years in your sight are like a day that has just gone by, or like a watch in the night." (NIV)

Albert Einstein demonstrated that time is not a constant. It is relative, depending on the speed of the observer. The faster we go, the more time slows down from our perspective. Time is also relative depending upon the proximity of an observer to a gravitational field. The closer we are and the more massive the body, the slower time proceeds from our perspective.

If we could compress the earth's mass down to an 18-inch sphere we would have a black hole. Ten inches out surrounding the sphere is the event horizon. Any light that passes by the event horizon will be pulled in by gravity and never, ever escape.

All time stops at the event horizon. According to Einstein, by definition, photons never degenerate. They just go on for eternity. Why? Because all time is stopped for a photon traveling at the speed of light.

The reason I mention this is because of the implications for an eternal heaven. Heaven time will just go on and on and on!

According to string theory, our universe exists in 11 dimensions—or possibly 24. In either case, the mathematical calculations are staggering. Passing through both the 11th and 26th dimensions, everything becomes a single point. This scientific observation may give us some small insight into the omnipresence of God! This may be one way He is everywhere all the time.

One day I got out my calculator and considered the relative perspective of time from God's point of view. According to Moses, if one day is with God as a thousand years, then one year on earth equals 86.4 seconds in heaven. Now, of course, this analogy is just for fun until we consider some rather intriguing implications regarding spiritual growth and time.

One of the most frequently asked questions I get from a new widow is, "Will he miss me?"

I respond to her with a sense of comfort and relief: "Let's put your question in perspective. Let's say you outlive your husband by ten years. Will he miss you? Well, if one year on earth equals 86.4 seconds in heaven, this means when your husband dies and goes to heaven, 15 minutes later, here you come! He's probably still waiting in line to see Jesus!" They always smile when I share that.

God is not in a hurry. It may seem our spiritual growth is proceeding slowly. God responds, "No, from my perspective, everything is right on schedule. I'm in no hurry. I am working for eternity."

Miles Stanford observed a fascinating insight culled from the writings and journals of some of the great Christian leaders of the past centuries. He mentioned some names like A. T. Pierson, Dwight L. Moody, Samuel Goforth, James McConkey, Andrew Murray, F. B. Meyer, Hudson Taylor, Ruth Paxon, and George Mueller:

The average for these was 15 years after they entered their life work before they began to know the Lord Jesus as their

Life, and ceased trying to work for Him and began allowing Him to be their all in all and to do His work through them.[31]

These results should not discourage us. Instead, they help us settle down and set our sights on eternity.

In *Principles of Spiritual Growth,* Miles Stanford quoted James Darby as saying, "It is God's design to set a new Christian aside for a while after his initial start, so that self-confidence may die down."[32] Too many new Christians start out on fire for Jesus, only to flame out shortly thereafter. Pacing is important.

The Apostle Paul became a Christian in his early thirties. Historical records corroborate that Paul was 49 when he embarked on his first missionary journey. The average male life expectancy in the first century was 35. In other words, Paul was an old man when he set sail.

For 17 years after his conversion God left Paul out in the desert, making tents, until Paul finally understood the victory belonged to God and not to Paul. Finally, at 49, Jesus said, "Okay, now I can use you. Let's go on a journey."

Too often, new Christians are told, "Now that you're a Christian, get to work. It's time for you to learn how to serve." It may well be that God has other ideas: "Hold it. Let him grow up a little bit. Let's put him aside for a while."

Julie and I were on vacation in Colorado when Brianna was a baby. On Sunday morning, we arrived late for church. No one was in sight—everyone was in Sunday School. Finally, we found the nursery. A young, 18- or 19-year-old girl was taking care of the babies. We placed Brianna in her care, and I asked, "Can you tell us where the Young Married Sunday School class is?"

She replied, "I don't know."

"You work in the Sunday School, and you don't know where the Young Married Sunday School class is?"

"I am sorry, I don't know. I just became a Christian last week, and they've got me in the nursery taking care of the babies!"

Unfortunately, this scenario is repeated all too often in the Christian church. She needed to be *in* a Sunday School Bible class, learning the foundations of the Christian life—not taking care of babies for other, more mature Christians.

God says to Christians in the initial stages of the journey, "Slow down. I'm in no hurry. Allow Me to take some time with you and let you grow up a bit before I launch you out into ministry.

A. W. Tozer was a Canadian who spent most of his ministry pastoring in Chicago. One of my favorite essays is his *The Inadequacy of Instant Christianity.*[33]

I'll paraphrase: "I want to thank you Americans for giving us instant coffee, instant television, and instant frozen dinners. Now, you've finally succeeded in bequeathing to the world instant Christianity. You have made it possible to walk down the aisle of a church, or pray a little prayer and say, 'I believe in Jesus,' and in 30 seconds you complete a divine transaction that makes you fit for heaven, and you never need to think about it again!"

It's no wonder we have so many little babies who never grow up.

What many Christians want, they want right now. Unfortunately, that mindset overflows into the spiritual realm. Spiritual growth is not a quick thing. Spiritual growth takes time. We cannot speed up the maturing process; however, we certainly can slow it down.

Some of you are thinking, "I've wasted a lot of years. I'm 45, I'm 50, or I'm 60-years old. I'm still a spiritual baby. I don't have enough time left to make it to maturity."

I say to you, "Don't be discouraged. You just might be surprised at what God can do with the rest of your life. It is never too late to begin!

> It takes God 100 years to make a mighty oak. He can turn out a squash in six weeks.[34]

3. It's not possible to commit suicide by self-crucifixion.

When's the last time you heard that someone committed suicide by crucifixion? You never have. It can't be done! People shoot themselves, take overdoses of pills, hurtle their cars into bridge abutments, slit their wrists, jump off cliffs, sit in their closed garages with the car engine running, and detonate suicide bombs—just to name a few of the morbid ways people commit suicide. But you never, ever, ever hear someone committed suicide by crucifixion. It can't be done!

An important spiritual growth principle says we can never design our own spiritual growth crucifixion. In Ephesians 2:10, Paul wrote:

> *"We are God's handiwork, created in Christ Jesus to do good works, which God prepared in advance for us to do." (NIV)*

In Philippians 2:13, Paul wrote:

> *"It is God who works in you to will and to act in order to fulfill his good purpose." (NIV)*

Crucifixion is God's work. Not ours. He has a plan and purpose at work in our lives. He will consummate his plan as He molds us to look like Christ.

The way to maturity is not to make problems for ourselves in an effort to speed up our spiritual growth. No! We don't crucify ourselves. We don't engineer our own spiritual processing. Some Christians are open, submissive, and desiring His work in their lives. Those He need only bend a little. Others have so much pride and self-dependence that God has much breaking in store for them.

My children are quite different. When my daughter Brianna got into trouble, often just a quick look and a scowl brought tears. She needed only slight bending. My youngest daughter Bronwyn was not at all like that. When she was in trouble, a quick look and a scowl often produced a quick look and a scowl right back. We had to do some breaking to overcome her little rebellious spirit.

Not everyone is called to bring down fire on Mt. Carmel. God-engineered crucifixion means the Father uses different methods and approaches in line with His purposes. I mentioned earlier I had a litany of God-designed training experiences including open-heart surgery; large intestine excision; a dead daughter; personal threats of bodily harm, and emotional upheavals.

How He molds me is not the same way He intends to mold you. You have your own trials. If I were to give you a chance in my class, you could easily share a litany of experiences God is using on you.

Many of you would listen to my story and say, "That's worse than what I've experienced!" Others of you would say, "That's not nearly as bad as what I've endured." That's the point! God uses different processes because His plan for us is personal—therefore, the process varies. Don't forget that some of us need only a little bending while others may need hard breaking.

What Needs to Die

Now, we must be clear on what it is God is crucifying. He has no intention of putting to death the essence of who we are. He keeps our personalities intact. Our pride, which manifests as self-reliance, self-centeredness, and self-condemnation is what He wants to kill. Pride is simply an over concern with myself.

Some use the term, "death to self" to describe the idea that when we are finally fully dead to self—our self is totally out of the way— we are finally able to reach the mountain peaks of maturity. Nothing is further from the truth. "Death to self" means putting aside self-reliance, self-centeredness, and self-condemnation.

John the Baptist said about Jesus:

> " *He must become greater; I must become less." John 3:30 (NIV)*

Our experience upward in the power of Christ is in direct proportion to our experience downward in ceasing from self.

Miles Stanford wrote:

> *In preparation there must be a tearing down before there can be a building up. ... It is more than comforting to realize that it is those who have plumbed the depths of failure to whom God invariably give the call to shepherd others. This is not a call given to the gifted, the highly trained, or the polished as such.... It takes a man who has discovered something of the measures of his own weakness to be patient with the foibles of others.*[35]

Bamboo

An old Chinese proverbial story explains God's processing and purpose.

Once upon a time, far off in the heart of the Western Kingdom, the master came to walk day by day. In the midst of the garden in the Western Kingdom was the most beautiful bamboo tree that ever grew in all the earth. The master would come by and look at his plants; but he had a special affinity for that old bamboo tree. He watched it as it grew. He nurtured it almost to complete maturity.

One day, as the great master was walking through his garden, he came to that bamboo tree, and on impulse that bamboo tree bowed down in loving adoration of his master. The master said, "Bamboo, most beautiful of all the trees in my garden, I think you're just about ready to become useful to me."

Bamboo said, "Oh, great master, if I can do anything for you, I will. Just take me. Use me."

The great master said, "Bamboo, Bamboo, most beautiful of all the trees in my garden, if I'm going to use you, I have to cut you down." The wind stopped blowing, and the birds stopped singing and all the butterflies were still.

Then Bamboo said, "Well, master, I'm yours. But you yourself said I'm the most beautiful of all the trees in the garden. Must you cut me down?"

"I must, if you're going to be useful to me." The sounds of the garden were hushed in silence as that great bamboo bent his neck, and the master cut him down.

Then the master said, "Bamboo, you're still not useful to me. If you're going to be useful to me, I must cut off all your branches."

Bamboo pleaded, "Oh, master, not that. You've already cut me down. Isn't that enough? Please don't cut off my branches."

But the great master said, "I must cut off your branches." Once more the garden was silenced, and all the plants looked on with rapt attention as the great master snipped off branch after branch and bared that great bamboo.

Then the master said, "Bamboo, you're not useful to me yet. There's one more thing. If you're going to be useful to me, then I must split you open and cut your heart out."

Bamboo wept, "Oh, master, not that! You've already taken away my beauty. There's nothing left now—just me. Must you scrape my heart out?"

"I must if you're to be useful to me.'" Once more the garden was hushed as the great master took that bamboo, split him down the middle and scraped his heart out.

Then the great master took that bamboo tree, now hollowed out and scraped clean, and walked over to a spring bubbling with water. He laid one end of that hollowed-out bamboo tree in the stream. He placed the other end of that bamboo tree in the irrigation ditch that watered his garden. Then the waters began to flow; and the fields began to grow. The wind began to blow again. The birds began to sing. The rice was planted, and the harvest came. And that bamboo who, standing all alone in the garden was the most beautiful of all the master's plants, that bamboo, which meant so much to himself, when he was stripped bare and hollowed out, was then, and only then, useful in the great master's garden.

Have you ever said to God, "I surrender my all to you. Just take me and use me"?

Did you mean it? Did you realize the implications of your surrender? Can you look back over your life and see the hand of God at work molding and sculpting in order for you to reflect more and more the glory of Christ? We want the touch of His hand on display in our lives for all the world to see.

> *So, bow your head. Go ahead. Ask God to continue molding you as a spiritual mother or father at any price. Ask Him to put to death the pride, self-reliance, self-centeredness, and self-condemnation that are death to living the Christian life.*
>
> *Now, once more, pray the prayer you know God guarantees He will answer.*
>
> *Amen.*

CHAPTER NINE

INTIMACY

Spiritual maturity moves us steadily toward an intimate relationship with God and with others.

"Tell me how you proposed to her," I asked the 46-year-old ex-con pastor. The reason he hadn't already married was because he had spent too many years in prison for a youthful indiscretion. He met Christ in prison, felt called to preach, attended school, and subsequently met the woman of his dreams.

He replied, "About 11:00 p.m. after an evening out together, I took her to the church. I told her to be obedient and go into the restroom and take off her nylons."

I was immediately uncomfortable with where this tale was heading.

"She was obedient," he continued. "I invited her to accompany me to the front of the sanctuary. We sat for a moment on the platform steps and then I reached for the basin of water and a towel I had previously placed under the front pew. As I began to wash her feet, I gazed into her eyes and said, "The most humble service Jesus ever did was to wash His disciples' feet. I want to wash your feet for the rest of your life." She was crying as I put down the towel, reached for the ring and asked, 'Will you marry me?'"

There may be better ways for a man to propose marriage to a woman—but certainly not many.

Intimate Friends

Intimacy is Jesus washing His disciples' feet, encouraging them to wash one another's feet and then declaring in John 15:15:

"I no longer call you servants, because a servant does not know his master's business. Instead, I have called you friends, for everything that I learned from my Father I have made known to you." (NIV)

No secrets now separated Jesus from His disciples. He has shared everything. Now they are the closest of friends.

Intimacy occurs when someone enters our world and feels what we feel, and experiences what we experience, and knows us like we know ourselves.[36]

Intimacy is Jesus in the upper room declaring:

"Greater love has no one than this: to lay down one's life for one's friends." John 15:13 (NIV)

Can you imagine Jesus looking into your eyes and saying, "I want to care for you, love you, and have an intimate relationship with you for the rest of your life?" Well, imagine it. It's true.

"The Lord is compassionate and gracious, slow to anger, abounding in love. ... For as high as the heavens are above the earth, so great is his love for those who fear him; . . . As a father has compassion on his children, so the Lord has compassion on those who fear him; for he knows how we are formed, he remembers that we are dust. Psalm 103:8, 11, 13 (NIV)

Bargaining For Souls

The angel of the Lord is a "theophany," a manifestation of Jesus in the Old Testament. Three angels appeared to Abraham and announced he and Sarah would soon have a child. The three heavenly creatures then turned toward Sodom and Gomorrah. Their next mission was to destroy these cities whose wickedness rose as a stench in the nostrils of God. As they prepared to leave the Lord said, *"Shall I hide from Abraham what I am about to do?" Genesis 18:17 (NIV)* James records their relationship like this:

"And the scripture was fulfilled that says, 'Abraham believed God, and it was credited to him as righteousness,' and he was called God's friend." James 2:23 (NIV)

How could God keep a secret from His friend Abraham? (Genesis 18:22)? He couldn't! A long discussion ensued as Abraham pleaded with the Lord for the salvation of the cities of the plain:

"Surely, you won't kill the righteous with the wicked. That is not like you! If there are 50 righteous people in the city, will you spare it?"

The Lord replied, "If I find 50 righteous, I will not destroy it for the sake of the 50."

"Will you spare them if there are only 45 righteous?"

"All right, for the sake of 45, I will not destroy them."

"Forty?'

"OK."

"Thirty?"

"OK."

"Twenty?"

"OK."

"Ten?"

"OK. For the sake of ten, I will not destroy it."

These two are close friends engaging in an open discussion about the next move of the angel of the Lord. The Lord must be quite intimate with Abraham to allow him to talk so freely to Him.

What if God were so close to you that He would not act without first telling you His intentions? Imagine being so close to God that He is willing to consider changing His plans because of what you might say. Abraham had the audacity to tell God he might lose face with unbelievers if He destroyed the righteous with the unrighteous. The Lord not only listened to His friend, He responded to Abraham's reasoning!

Enoch was an early patriarch who was intimate with God. In Genesis 5:22-24 we learn that Enoch walked closely with God and when he was 365 years old, "he was no more, because God took him away." (NIV) Apparently, Enoch and God enjoyed sweet fellowship. Once, at the end of a long walk together, apparently Enoch said, "Well, it's getting late, I had better be getting back home."

God replied, "It is such a long way back to your house. Why don't you just come on home with me?"

"All right, I think I will." Enoch's experience helps us to better understand Psalm 116:15:

> *"Precious in the sight of the LORD is the death of his faithful servants." (NIV)*

Eternal Life

Jesus was only hours away from the cross when He prayed His high priestly prayer on behalf of His disciples:

> *"Now this is eternal life: that they may know you, the only true God, and Jesus Christ, whom you have sent. . . I will remain in the world no longer, but they are still in the world, and I am coming to you. Holy Father, protect them by the power of your name, the name you gave me, so that they may be one as we are one." John 17:3 and 11 (NIV)*

For many Christians the term, "eternal life," describes living forever in heaven. Eternal life to most people is a length of time. However, it has a deeper meaning. To Jesus, eternal life is an increasingly, deepening relationship with God the Father and God the Son. Eternal life is a function of intimacy. Have you ever contemplated the reason for mankind's existence? We all wonder, why are we here? What is the purpose of the creation? Where did life come from?

Have you ever considered the reason for life on earth is that God doesn't like to be alone? We are created in God's image (Genesis 1:26). Certainly, fellowship and intimacy exist among the three persons of the Trinity. While being three, God is also One. Perhaps we don't like to be alone because God does not like being alone either.

God said to Adam: *"It is not good for man to be alone." Genesis 2:18 (NIV)* How did God know that? Of course, since God is omniscient, He knows everything. However, perhaps the answer is more emotionally complex. Has God ever experienced aloneness? Listen to the horror of anguished desolation as Jesus spoke from the cross.

> *"My God, my God, why have you forsaken me?" Matthew 27:46 (NIV)*

Consider that God's primary purpose for creation was to establish a relationship with mankind. As a result of the fall, His primary purpose now is to restore our broken relationship with Him.

The Bible is filled with examples of God's emotions. As we have just seen, loneliness is one of them.

There are many others:

> *"The Lord <u>regretted</u> that he had made human beings on the earth, and his heart was <u>deeply troubled</u>. So the Lord said, "I will wipe from the face of the earth the human race I have created." Genesis 6:6-7 (NIV)*
>
> *"For God so <u>loved</u> the world that he gave his only son . . ." John 3:16. (RSV)*

When the rich young ruler turned away, Jesus "looked at him and loved him" as He watched him walk away. Mark 10:21 (NIV)

We see grief, pain, anger, love, and compassion all in the above verses. Throughout the Scriptures the many emotions of God the Father are put on display.

Julie and I were driving to Phoenix to attend a marriage retreat for pastors—and I didn't want to go. The pressure of people and job responsibilities had gotten to me. I was burned out and overwhelmed.

I told Julie, "The last thing I want to do is go to a marriage retreat with a group of pastors and wives. I just want to get away alone. If I could have several days off by myself, I think I could get my feet back on the ground." (You can imagine how much this hurt Julie.)

I proceeded to tell Julie I had no intention of engaging in any of the sessions. I intended to work on my sermon for Sunday morning. The notes were resting in my pocket.

When the session began, I pulled out my notes and immediately went to work on my sermon. About 15 minutes into David Ferguson's lecture, he quoted Genesis 2:18:

> *"The LORD God said, 'It is not good for the man to be alone.'" (NIV)*

I wonderedThat got my attention. I I wondered, "Is he messing with my plan?" I decided to listen for 15 more minutes and then return to my sermon. After 15 minutes I was so intrigued that my sermon notes never came out of my pocket again.

Loneliness

God made clear that oneness with Him alone is not enough. Man needs God; but he needs others, too. Many times, I've heard Christians say, "All I need is Jesus!" But according to God, that's just not true. If all we have is Jesus, that is not enough.

No one need go on the spiritual journey alone.

The ranks of Christendom are filled with those who long to quench their spiritual thirst. Find some of those Christians and spend time with them.

God's declaration that it is not good for man to be alone is not just a situational necessity, it is an eternal truth.

Too often we're taught that mankind's problems began when Eve ate the fruit as recorded in Genesis 3:1-24. However, Adam's and Eve's problems began long before that in Genesis 2 while they were still perfect. They were already in trouble. They were alone.

God's solution to loneliness is found in relationships. God declared in the next part of Genesis 2:18: "I will make a helper suitable for him." (NIV) The primary reason for marriage is to remove aloneness. The primary purpose of any relationship is to minister to another's aloneness.

Adam broke not only his relationship with God, but also God's heart when he ate the forbidden fruit and entered into the world of sin:

> "Then the man and his wife heard the sound of the LORD God as he was walking in the garden in the cool of the day, and they hid from the LORD God among the trees of the garden. But the LORD God called to the man, 'Where are you?'"
> Genesis 3:8-9 (NIV)

Do you hear the care, concern, and disappointment in God's voice? When you read the entire passage, you see that God was looking forward to His daily communion with Adam and Eve. However, they were hiding, afraid to face God. Intimacy was gone. Their relationship with their Creator was marred forever.

"Where are you, Adam?"

What was God thinking as He asked this soul-searching question: "Are you lying hurt or injured somewhere? Have you gotten tired of me? Have you found something else more fulfilling than I? Have you eaten the fruit I told you not to eat?"

Do you hear the hurt in God's heart? God would not meet with Adam in the Garden again. However, He immediately initiated a plan to restore mankind to the open and vulnerable friendship he once had with Adam before the fall.

"All this is from God, who reconciled us to himself through Christ and gave us the ministry of reconciliation: that God was reconciling the world to himself in Christ, not counting people's sins against them." 2 Corinthians 5:18-19 (NIV)

Let's reiterate the outline of 1 John 2:12-14. Remember, this passage reveals a progression in our friendship with God.

Spiritual children experience the beginnings of a relationship in their initial encounters with Jesus. They are little more than acquaintances with Him.

Spiritual young men and women are well acquainted with the indwelling Christ. They are strong. They know the word of God. They have overcome the evil one.

Spiritual mothers and fathers are intimate with God. John twice repeated the phrase, "you know him who is from the beginning," to communicate the depths of intimacy they had together.

Let's consider how deep intimacy might manifest. God hurts for us when we hurt. The people who know us best are the ones who know us in our pain. God knows our pain and we know Him in His. Our intimacy with Him knows deep depths of love.

What if your relationship with God were so close you sensed when He was crying for you when you hurt? Paul described this kind of intimacy:

> *"Praise be to the God and Father of our Lord Jesus Christ, the Father of compassion and the God of all comfort, who comforts us in all our troubles, so that we can comfort those in any trouble with the comfort we ourselves receive from God."*
> *2 Corinthians 1:3-4 (NIV)*

Unfortunately, I find many spiritual children read these words, but rarely experience them. On the other hand, spiritual mothers and fathers experience deeply God's comfort in all kinds of difficult situations.

Bronwyn

My youngest daughter, Bronwyn, spent a year in Germany as an exchange student. It was not an easy year. Julie and I were in London when Bronwyn flew over to spend the final week of her Christmas break with us. We knew the previous six months overseas were hard—but not how hard.

Three weeks before Bronwyn arrived in Germany the father of her host family was tragically killed in a chainsaw accident. Can you imagine the hurt and grief in her sponsor family? During her first week she traveled to Norway, where her host family picked out a casket and prepared for his funeral. Things went downhill from there. In a third-floor hotel room near Victoria Station in London, we were heartbroken as she poured forth misery, aloneness, and pain.

We tried to talk Bronwyn into coming home. But she steadfastly refused: "I will finish what I started."

We boarded different planes several days later, she to Hamburg and we to America. We wept as we waved good-bye.

Julie was crying as we waited for the airplane door to close. "I am sorry," I said to Julie. "I know this is really hurting you. It's hard to watch Bronwyn walk back into the fire."

Julie dried her tears and said, "No, you misunderstand. I am not crying about Bronwyn. I was crying because I felt Jesus weeping along with me."

Healthy relationships flow two ways. We like it when God comforts us. Did you ever stop to think God might like it when we comfort Him? Is this not what friends are for?

Orlando Girl

The young lady seated next to me on the airplane was *reading The Celestine Prophecy*. After appropriate introductions I said, "I see you're reading a book for Gen Xers who are on spiritual searches." She looked surprised that a man old enough to be her father might be familiar with a book targeting her generation.

"I would suppose," I said, "you're on a spiritual journey." She nodded slightly. "I would suppose," I continued, "you were wounded so deeply in some church you have decided never to return."

She was shocked: "How did you know that?"

"It's not hard. Many people in America have some sort of church or religious background. The fact you're reading *The Celestine Prophecy* tells me you're on some sort of a special search, and the reason many people search is because they were hurt by some church or religious people."

I call this type of ministering playing "spiritual hunch cards."

After several moments of silence, I said, "I'm sorry for what happened to you. I am sure it hurt a lot for you to pull up your spiritual roots and leave."

We sat in silence for several moments more. Finally, she said, "Would you like to know what happened?"

"OK."

"Four months ago, I gave birth to my baby, and she was stillborn. I begged and begged my priest to baptize her, but he wouldn't do it. He said the church didn't baptize dead babies. I was devastated. I'll never go back there." She happened to be from a Roman Catholic background, but what happened to her could—and too often does—happen in any church.

I have learned whenever I see hurt to try to comfort it (Matthew 5:4). So, I said to her, "I'm sorry. Did you know your baby was in trouble?"

"No. The cord was wrapped around her neck and by the time they realized it, she was gone."

"I am sorry. Life is not supposed to turn out like that. You must have felt so rejected."

She certainly did. I spent the next several minutes trying to comfort that pain.

"I know you had all sorts of dreams you imagined you would enjoy with her, and in an instant they were gone. My heart just breaks as I think about what you lost. You were worried about whether your baby was going to go to heaven, weren't you?"

She was sobbing quietly now. "I am sorry you had to worry about that. Fortunately, Jesus tells us that when little children die, they immediately go to heaven (Luke 10:14-16). Nevertheless, what a horrible moment that was for you. I grieve that this happened to you and your baby."

It was time to be quiet. I had said enough. We sat in silence again for a while. Presently, she said, "And, I guess the reason it hurt so much was because I have had four miscarriages."

I thought to myself, "She must be kidding!" I said softly, "You poor girl. I can't imagine all the emotional pain and suffering you have endured." Then, I said, "And, I imagine you went through all four miscarriages alone, didn't you?"

She looked at me.

"Oh, I know what happened. Your husband didn't get it, did he? You were all excited. A new life was growing within you. Your body was changing and suddenly, it was over. And he didn't get it, did he? I know he told you he was sorry. But he didn't have the same feelings you had, did he? He went on with life. You went on with grieving. Did you name the babies?"

She looked over at me, tears streaming down her cheeks and nodded. She had a name for each of the four. So, I comforted her four miscarriages worth of hurt.

I said to her, "You don't need to worry about your baby. Your baby is in heaven." I shared with her several passages that describe babies in heaven. When David's baby died, he said in 2 Samuel 12:23: *"But now that he is dead, why should I go on fasting? Can I bring him back again? I will go to him, but he will not return to me."*

In Mark 10:13-16 Jesus said:

> *"People were bringing little children to Jesus for him to place his hands on them, but the disciples rebuked them. When Jesus saw this, he was indignant. He said to them, "Let the little children come to me, and do not hinder them, for the kingdom of God belongs to such as these. . . . And he took the children in his arms, placed his hands on them and blessed them." (NIV)*

"Your baby is OK. She is in heaven," I said, "Would you like to talk about how you can be in heaven with her?"

She listened intently as I described the resurrection of Christ and talked about Jesus' promise that if we believed in Him, we could cheat death and live forever. Just before landing, she opened her heart and received Jesus on the basis of John 1:12 and entered into the kingdom of God.

Later that evening I spent time grieving with Jesus. Grieving with Jesus is an essential part of the spiritual process. Paul declared:

> *"I want to know Christ and the power of his resurrection and the fellowship of sharing in his sufferings, becoming like him in his death, and so, somehow, to attain to the resurrection from the dead" (Philippians 3:10-11).*

Notice the path to the resurrected life involves entering into the "fellowship of His sufferings." This is more than being physically persecuted for Jesus' sake. It includes engaging with Jesus in his spiritual and mental sufferings for hurting people throughout the world.

Comfort

What do grieving people need? Comfort! (Matthew 5:4). After all, what are friends for? We may hurt, grieve, and mourn alone, but we cannot comfort ourselves alone.

Based on all we have seen so far, there's no doubt God's feelings and hurts are healed as he mourns and is comforted by us.

So, when I reached my hotel, I prayed to comfort Jesus regarding the pain of *The Celestine Prophecy* girl: "I know you were hurting because she was hurting. You grieved when you saw her suffering alone. I know you wept as she was rejected. I know it broke your heart when she turned away from her relationship with you and began searching for someone other than you. I'm sorry you were brokenhearted because of all over the pain, loss, loneliness, and confusion in her life. I am so sorry you are grieving over her and her pain.

In Romans 12:15, Paul gave some great advice on how to minister to aloneness:

> *"Rejoice with those who rejoice; mourn with those who mourn." (NIV)*

After some time spent mourning with God, it was time for us to rejoice together. After all, a confused, searching, 28-year-old woman was back on track! We spent quite some time rejoicing!

A Hug

Don Graham shared a story about a woman named Linda who traveled alone up the rutted and rugged highway from Alberta, Canada to the Yukon. Linda didn't know you don't travel to Whitehorse alone in a rundown Honda Civic. So she set off where normally only four-wheel drives ventured.

The first evening she found an inn near a mountaintop and asked for a five a.m. wake-up call. She didn't understand why the clerk looked surprised at her request until she awoke the next morning to a thick fog enshrouding the mountain.

Not wanting to look foolish, she got up and went to breakfast. Two truckers invited her to join them and, since the place was so small and deserted, she felt obliged.

"Where are you headed," one trucker asked.

"Whitehorse."

"In that little Honda Civic! No way! The pass is dangerous in weather like this."

Well, I am determined to try," was Linda's gutsy, if rather ignorant response.

"Then, I guess we're just going to have to hug you," the trucker suggested.

Linda drew back, "There is no way I'm going to let you touch me!"

"Not like that!" both truckers chuckled. "We will put one truck in front of you and one in the rear. That's what we call 'hugging.' That's how to get you safely through the mountains."

As we go through the trials and troubles of life, we all need hugging. We don't want to go through life alone. We need an intimate relationship with God and with the people God has placed around us. Remember, while we need others, others need us, too.

Dear Father in heaven,

Please walk beside me on my spiritual journey. Help me find spiritually like-minded friends as I travel the road of spiritual maturity. Lead me as I enter into the "fellowship of your sufferings." I want to comfort you in your hurts as you have comforted me in mine.

Amen.

CHAPTER 10

SUFFERING

---

*We must see human suffering through
the lens of a biblical worldview.*

"I wanted to be the first to tell you. We made a mistake. I held your heart in the palm of my hand and cut it open to find the hole. But there was none. You have a perfect heart."

I knew God loved me. But why did I have to suffer so much? At the forefront of my 13-year-old mind loomed the age-old question: "If God is all loving and all-powerful, why does He allow such terrible pain and suffering in the world?"

Today I might pose the question differently: "How do we reconcile the theological conflict between an all-loving, all-powerful God and the undeniable suffering seemingly perpetrated by the God who created humanity?"

To properly answer this question, we need to be certain we have a biblical worldview.

Our worldview is how we see the world through all of our of cultural, philosophical, moral, ethical, and religious lenses. We use our worldviews to interpret life events. Worldviews deal with such issues as where God came from and what kind of God He is. A worldview explains the reasons for suffering and clarifies what happens after death. Our worldview is the basis for our value system and how we understand the meaning and purpose of life.

Let me give you some samples of what worldviews look like so we can better understand and craft our own.

George Barna identifies several non-biblical worldviews:

- *Deism: The Absent God.* God exists and created the universe, but has abandoned the world, letting it run its own course. godRelativism rules.

- *Naturalism: What You See Is What You Get.* God does not exist. History and humans have no purpose. Human choices are driven by survival.

- *Pantheism: Impersonal Divinity.* Everything is part of God. Pantheists seek to reach oneness with the universe.

- *New Age: Philosophical Syncretism.* There is no transcendent God and no evil power to oppose divine power or humanity. Individuals are exalted as the ultimate authorities and are viewed as divine. People can evolve to higher levels of consciousness through a series of personal and mystical experiences.

- *Post-modernism: Hyper-Individualism.* There is no grand story that explains life and reality. Personal experience becomes a relative truth that substitutes for absolute truth[37.]

Biblical Worldview

I will outline the biblical worldview in some detail. It explains why a loving God could allow pain and suffering on earth.

- The Bible is the inspired, inerrant Word of God.

- Absolute truths do exist.

- God is transcendent, omnipresent (everywhere, all the time), omnipotent (all-powerful) and omniscient (knows all things).

- God created the heavens and the earth. Everything has its origin in His creation.

- Man was created in the image of God. Man is not God, nor can he become a god. Jesus is 100 percent God and 100 percent human (the hypostatic union).

- Unfortunately, mankind was deceived and led into sin by Satan.

- Jesus died a substitutionary death on the cross to provide forgiveness for man's sin. All who believe in Him by faith alone have their sins forgiven and enjoy a right and eternal relationship with God the Father. Those who choose not to believe in Christ are eternally separated from God in hell for eternity.

- The world is a fallen world. The Kingdom of God is not now on earth. As a Matthew 5:4result, natural catastrophes, wars, murders, stealing, accidents, failures, and poor decisions, are often the expected results of a fallen world waiting to be redeemed by Christ. [38]
- Satan, not God, is the instigator of the pain, troubles, and suffering in the world.
- The commandments and instructions of Scripture provide the foundation for Christian morality and ethics.

At this present time, Satan holds sway over the earth (Luke 4:5-7). This is why Jesus told us to pray, *"your kingdom come, your will be done, on earth as it is in heaven."* Matthew 6:10 (NIV)

The Book of Revelation declares Satan now owns the title deed to the earth—only Jesus is worthy to take it back (Revelation 5:5). Revelation is the story of how Jesus regains the Kingdom. Someday, when the events of the Book of Revelation are fulfilled, we will no longer contend with pain and suffering. Life will then work the way we wish it would—and the way God initially designed it to be. But not now. Not yet.

As Christians, we must accept the reality of the biblical worldview. Just because we don't like it, we dare not conceive of some alternative worldview that imagines the world to work the way we think it should. An improper worldview will only bring disappointment when things don't work out the way we imagine they should.

Early in my ministry I put together a personal checklist of most of the biblical reasons for suffering. The checklist in my early ministry had only three questions.

I've now expanded my checklist to ten. These questions presuppose a biblical worldview and are designed for us to use when we experience a personal suffering.

Question One: Is this sickness or suffering the result of the fallen world order in which we live?

....

....

....

The fall of Adam introduced sickness, colds, cancer, rape, accidents, pinched sciatic nerves, death, and everything we call evil. These are realities of our fallen world.

One of our Wycliffe Bible Translators went into anaphylactic shock immediately following an insect bite. By the time he was airlifted to the hospital, the oxygen loss to his brain meant likely brain damage and probable death.

When I arrived to pray with the family, I sensed in my spirit this sickness was the misfortune of a broken world. So, I prayed accordingly: "Lord, there is no reason for this sickness to end in death. He needs to finish his Bible translation. He has children to raise. This is not the time to die. Heal him and make him well."

This prayer illustrates what James referred to as the "prayer offered in faith" in James 5:15. Faith always begins with a word from God. Once His will is revealed it is easy to pray in faith.

Several days later the family asked our church elders to anoint him with oil and pray for his healing according to James 5:14-16. With his doctor's permission, our elders entered the intensive care unit. We all felt strongly from God that this sickness was not unto death. So, we anointed him with oil and prayed in faith for his healing. Three hours later he was sitting up in bed eating. Today, his children are grown up and his translation is finished.

Of course, not all trials have good endings. The first teenager I buried was driving home when a drunk driver crossed the median and killed him. According to a biblical worldview, this accident was most definitely not God's will. It was an accidental occurrence in a sinful and fallen world.

Question Two: Is it time to die?

....

....

....

"Roger, please come, Karl is dying."

When I arrived, Wally and Cosetta, Bill and Fran, and Ann were gathered around the hospital bed in Karl's living room. Karl had awakened early that morning and asked his wife, 'Grace, what day is it?'

"Saturday."

"Is it a good day to go home to the Lord?"

"Any day is a good day to go home to the Lord."

"Then, I think I'll go today."

His lungs were rapidly filling with fluid. In a soft voice Karl began to sing, "Jesus loves me this I know, for the Bible tells me so…"

I thought to myself, "It doesn't get more lovely and tender than this."

"Roger, please read 2 Corinthians 5 to me."

So, I did:

> *For we know that if the earthly tent we live in is destroyed, we have a building from God, an eternal house in heaven, not built by human hands. Meanwhile we groan, longing to be clothed instead with our heavenly dwelling … so that what is mortal may be swallowed up by life. … Therefore we are always confident and know that as long as we are at home in the body we are away from the Lord. For we live by faith, not by sight. We are confident, I say, and would prefer to be away from the body and at home with the Lord. 2 Corinthians 5:1-8 (NIV)*

"I am ready to go see Jesus now."

"OK, Karl. Why don't you just close your eyes and go?"

An hour later he did.

The day will come when our lives will be closed like a book and the last chapter written. Then, thank God, we have faith to know He will lead us into glory.

I remember asking God, "Is our daughter Jessie's sickness unto death?"

He gently answered, "Yes."

Shortly after Jessie was born, a woman approached me and said, "If you just had enough faith your daughter would be healed." She was well meaning but ignorant. It is not always God's will to heal. Sometimes it is time to die.

Sometimes people want to die but the time is not right. Late one night I made a trip to the emergency room to pray for an elderly woman having a heart attack. We were long-time friends. Her husband had recently died after a long illness. As I bent over the gurney she whispered, "Roger, please pray for me to die. I miss Stretch so much. I want to go to heaven and be with Him."

I was deeply conflicted. Since when does a pastor pray for his parishioner to die? Finally, I decided, "Why not? She has lived a long and fruitful life. She misses her husband. If this is not her time, it is probably close to it."

So, I bowed my head and prayed for God to let her die. I opened my eyes and found myself face to face with the doctor assigned to treat her. He smiled and winked. He understood.

Question Three: Is this suffering a punishment because of a sin I've committed?

....

....

....

Sometimes a difficult circumstance or severe illness is a form of God's discipline. Paul described this as "reproof" or "correction" in 2 Timothy 2:2.

Miriam (Numbers 12:1-15), Uzziah (2 Chronicles 26:16-21), and Gehazi (2 Kings 5:26-27) were all struck with leprosy because of their sins.

Jesus said to the man at the Pool of Siloam, "Stop sinning or something worse may happen to you" (John 5:14).

Ananias and Sapphira were struck down by the Holy Spirit for lying (Acts 5:1-10).

The consequences of the sins of the fathers can be passed on to their children to the fourth generation (Exodus 20:5-6).

Some of the Corinthians who desecrated the Lord's Supper in 1 Corinthians 11:27-30 were sick and some were dead because of their ungodly behavior.

Have I seen people suffer sickness because of their sins? I believe, yes.

I pondered this third question as I searched my heart regarding Jessie: "Lord Jesus, is Jessie's sickness the punishment for some sin I have committed?" I thought of my many sins. If God wanted to punish me with a dying daughter, He had plenty of justification.

But, as I prayed, I sensed the calm, quiet voice of the Holy Spirit whisper from deep within, "No, this is not punishment for sin."

Question Four: Is this trial the result of some spiritual battle in the spirit realm?

....

....

....

Job endured horrible tragedies and sicknesses. He suffered because of the battle taking place between God and Satan in the spiritual realm. Of the many lessons we learn from Job's experience two things stand out.

First, many of the battles we face on earth are the result of the eternal struggle behind the scenes in the spirit realm between God and Satan. What happens in heaven is played out as spiritual battles on earth.

Second, many of our spiritual battles are fought over whether we accept the difficulties we face. When we handle our struggles without murmuring and complaining God gets glory from how we respond.

Job's experience in the physical realm mirrored the ongoing struggle between God and Satan in the spiritual realm. Job was just a suffering pawn in the chess match of heaven (Job 1-2). Unfortunately, he never figured out what was really going on.

> The Lord said to Satan, "Have you considered my servant Job? There is no one on earth like him; he is blameless and upright, a man who fears God and shuns evil."
>
> "Does Job fear God for nothing?" Satan replied. "Have you not put a hedge around him and his household and everything he has? You have blessed the work of his hands, so that his flocks and herds are spread throughout the land. But stretch out your hand and strike everything he has, and he will surely curse you to your face."

The Lord said to Satan, "Very well then, everything he has is in your power, but on the man himself do not lay a finger." Job 1:8-12 (NIV)

Then Satan went out from the presence of the Lord and killed Job's children. Job then lost his oxen, his donkeys, his sheep, his camels, and his servants.

"At this, Job got up and tore his robe and shaved his head. Then, he fell to the ground in worship and said: 'Naked I came from my mother's womb and naked I will depart. The Lord gave and the Lord has taken away; may the name of the Lord be praised.'" Job 1:21 (NIV)

Shortly after Jessie died, I was going for my spiritual checklist and came to the one on spiritual warfare. Deep in my spirit I heard God say, "Of course it's spiritual warfare. She's part of the struggle."

Thinking back now after over 60 years of ministry, I can see so many victories as Julie and I have labored in the kingdom. I also see that every one of the spiritual struggles we faced are also faced by every believer. Oftentimes, the wars occurring on earth are simply reflections of what's going on in heaven between God and Satan.

Now, when we sense the battle raging in the spiritual realm, we know better how to overcome the evil one as James instructs us in James 4:7: *Submit yourselves, then, to God. Resist the devil, and he will flee from you." (NIV)*

The spiritual warfare on earth manifests itself in numerous ways. Perhaps there is a battle over the soul of a person who needs find Jesus as personal Savior. Paul tells us, *"The god of this age [Satan] has blinded the minds of unbelievers, so that they cannot see the light of the gospel that displays the glory of Christ, who is the image of God." 2 Corinthians 4:4 (NIV)*

Satan is known as the accuser of the brethren. The battle is to be the kind of Christian God wants us to be.

Of course, Satan is the father of all lies. We must be careful to let truth and truth alone entered our minds.

He is actively placing great temptations designed to ruin ourselves and our relationship to God.

He is the master of deceit. He deceived Eve in the garden and if we are not careful, he will deceive us, too. If Satan was able to deceive perfect Eve, then be warned, none of us is perfect. We had better be very careful in our dealings with him!

Question Five: Is this suffering designed to bring God glory?

....

....

....

Before Jesus healed the man born blind, His disciples asked Him, "Rabbi, who sinned, this man or his parents, that he was born blind?" John 9:2 (NIV)

Jesus responded, "Neither this man nor his parents sinned . . . but this happened so that the works of God might be displayed in him." John 9:3 (NIV)

As a result of the blind man's suffering, his healing still gives Jesus glory some 2,000 years later.

Psalm 50 declares that when God does a remarkable miracle, the proper response is to tell everyone in the sanctuary about it. God is glorified in the retelling of the testimony.

God receives glory from the way we respond during our troubles. When we murmur, complain, gripe, and get angry at God, there is not much glory revealed. But let us live out Philippians 4:10-13—and be content in every circumstance because Jesus Christ is pouring in the power. Then glory is everywhere.

God reveals his glory as we live love-filled Christian lives. People are always watching and when we live a lovely, attractive life there are people who see what we have and would like to have it, too.

When Jessie's life ended three months short of a year, I asked Jesus if her short life would bring Him glory. I felt God was saying, "Yes, the focus of your ministry will be on helping little spiritual babies grow up. I plan on your life and ministry bringing me glory for many years to come."

I hope Jesus has received much glory from those I've tried to encourage to become spiritual mothers and fathers at any price.

Question Six: Is this suffering designed to refine and mature me to be more like Christ?

....

....

....

Job was engaged in the refining process when he declared: *"But he knows the way that I take; when he has tested me, I will come forth as gold." Job 23:10 (NIV)* All suffering can be used by God to make us more like Christ, whether it is God-designed or the natural result of a fallen world. A little reflection often unveils His hand at work in every trouble.

The secret police in a Middle Eastern country called in one of our national missionary friends for questioning. When the police seated her, she felt Jesus say, "You are in charge of this conversation."

So, she took the initiative: "Relax, guys. We know why we're here. Let's get on with the interrogation."

The interrogator then actually surprised our friend by apologizing: "I'm sorry. It's my first time to interrogate a Christian."

Our friend replied: "That's okay. I'll help you."

They began with a basic set of questions. Then, finally, they got to the heart of the matter: "Why have you become a Christian?"

She shared the Gospel and then said, "I'm telling you God loves you and has a wonderful plan for your life." They were stunned by her boldness as she continued with the story of the Prodigal Son.

Then she shared her personal testimony: "Let me tell you what Christ did for me. I hated myself. I hated this country. I hated the police. After I received Jesus, He showed me my worth. He gave me a love for your country. He even gave me a love for you, because inside your uniform is a man with needs, fears, and questions. You are a man Jesus is waiting to love."

Astonishingly, when she finished, the police interrogator said, "Thank you. I have never heard anybody talk about God this way." Years of suffering and fear had finally produced in her such a Christlikeness that she was even talking like Jesus.

Question Seven: Is this suffering the result of following Christ?

....

....

....

Jesus declared the Christian manifesto of suffering as He finished the Beatitudes:

> *"Blessed are you when people insult you, persecute you and falsely say all kinds of evil against you because of me. Rejoice and be glad, because great is your reward in heaven, for in the same way they persecuted the prophets who were before you." Matthew 5:11-12 (NIV)*

The early Apostles understood the relationship between suffering and following Jesus: *"The apostles left the Sanhedrin, rejoicing because they had been counted worthy of suffering disgrace for the Name." Acts 5:41 (NIV)*

Paul viewed suffering for Jesus as a treasured pleasure:

> *"For it has been granted to you on behalf of Christ not only to believe in him, but also to suffer for him ..." Philippians 1:29 (NIV)*

Another missionary couple in a Middle Eastern country was called in by the secret police in order to force them to reveal the names of other Christians living in their country. They were placed in separate rooms. The husband was interrogated and tortured when he refused to divulge names. They burned the soles of his feet with lighted cigarette butts, but he still refused. Finally, a curtain drew back and through the one-way glass he saw four men in the next room with his naked wife tied to a chair.

"Tell us what we want to know, or we'll take turns raping your wife." Our friend refused. He was forced to watch as they raped his wife. Later both were finally released. The names of the Christians there are still unknown to the secret police.

I asked them how they did it. The wife said, "We made a vow that we would protect our Christian friends even if it cost of our lives."

I said, "I've always believed forgiveness is a process. How long did it take for you to forgive them?"

"We forgave them immediately. If we didn't, we'd never be able to accomplish our ministries."

Frankly, I cannot conceive of the faith and God-given strength of these missionary men and women who stand strong for Jesus during intense persecution. No wonder there are so many rewards in heaven promised for those who suffer and die for Christ.

Question Eight: Is this suffering the result of doing good?

....

....

....

Peter encouraged goodness and integrity even if it brought pain. He wrote in 1 Peter 3:17: *"It is better, if it is God's will, to suffer for doing good than for doing evil." (NIV)*

My father worked for the same airline company for 40 years. Shortly after new management moved in, every officer in the company was let go. My father was in surgery when a morning newspaper article appeared announcing his replacement.

Dad had no desire to retire, but he was tossed out. He told me, "Someday, when (he named the new leader of the company) is burning in hell and God tells me to dip my finger in the water and bring him a drop, I am not going to do it."

Dad was so angry. Over time, he slowly processed the hurt and eventually forgave the man.

Two years later, two FBI agents knocked on dad's door and invited themselves in. They wanted to know about some transactions that occurred after my dad left the company. It seems the Feds had discovered a secret slush fund siphoning money to President Nixon's reelection campaign. Before dad's involuntary retirement, he oversaw the company finances. He was a man of integrity—and the new management knew he would never go along with the deception and so he needed to be removed. He suffered for doing good.

But there was a silver lining. Dad said often the best day of his life was the day he was dismissed. He started his own accounting business. When he reached 65, he decided it was time to work only in the morning and play golf in the afternoon. When he reached 70, he decided to close down the accounting business and just play golf. He often said, "I would never have seen 65 had I not gotten out of that stressful situation." My brother and I buried him when he was 85.

Question Nine: Is this suffering intended to keep me from future sin?

....

....

....

Sometimes it is! Think about Paul's thorn:

> *"To keep me from becoming conceited, I was given a thorn in my flesh, a messenger of Satan, to torment me. Three times I pleaded with the Lord to take it away from me. But he said to me, 'My grace is sufficient for you, for my power is made perfect in weakness." 2 Corinthians 12:7-9 (NIV)*

Question Ten: Is this suffering designed to increase my God dependence?

....

....

....

Early on, the disciples didn't know what to think of Jesus. So He engineered a three-and-a-half year training program aimed at increasing their God dependence. The storm on the Sea of Galilee was part of the training:

> *Then he got into the boat and his disciples followed him. Suddenly a furious storm came up on the lake, so that the waves swept over the boat. But Jesus was sleeping. The disciples went and woke him, saying, "Lord, save us! We're going to drown!"*
>
> *He replied, "You of little faith, why are you so afraid?" Then he got up and rebuked the winds and the waves, and it was completely calm.*

The men were amazed and asked, "'What kind of man is this? Even the winds and the waves obey him!" Matthew 8:23-27 (NIV)

Julie and I sat with a Christian missionary couple who had been shot at and threatened by Shiite extremists in their Middle Eastern country. One of their Christian compatriots recently had four bullets removed from his leg.

Every morning they walked their ten-year-old daughter to school. Throughout the day they heard mortar fire pummeling buildings just blocks away. Every morning they prayed for her school to still be standing when they picked up their daughter later that day.

We asked them how they had the courage to stay in a nation of anarchy and chaos. After all, the wife has her doctorate from Oxford in chemistry and her husband has his Ph.D. from Oxford in architecture. They could have had successful business careers anywhere in the world. Before the husband came to Christ, he was one of the wealthiest businessmen in his country. Unfortunately, since coming to Christ they were rejected in their hometown and hunted by Shi'ite fundamentalists.

Nevertheless, they decided to remain instead of fleeing. Why? Because Jesus had so changed their lives, they now wanted to be catalysts for Christ. So, day after day, in the ruins of the city, they help with emergency medical care, trauma counseling—and leading people to Christ. Their God dependence soared!

"How do you do this?" Julie asked.

"Well, you know the answer to that," she said through our translator, "we live every day in total dependence on God and His grace."

Our biblical worldview regarding suffering produces several helpful life sustaining applications.

Application One: We are sometimes forced to live with mystery!

Paul wrote: *"Now we see only a reflection as in a mirror; then we shall see face to face. Now I know in part; then I shall know fully, even as I am fully known." 1 Corinthians 13:12 (NIV)* We will learn all the answers later.

I enjoy those passages when Christ had to admit, "I don't know everything!"

The disciples asked, "When will your coming be?" Jesus was forced to say, "I don't know."

One day James and John asked, "Can we sit, one on your right and one on the left?" Jesus said, "That's not mine to give." It was a mystery to Him.

I heard Calvin Miller tell a "once upon a time" story about a traveler who saw a monastery up ahead in the dim rainy mist. He knocked on the door and when the abbot answered, he asked, "May I come in?"

The abbot said, "Not only may you come in, you may eat with us."

He had a wonderful evening, safe, dry, well fed, and warm. Because the weather was so bad, the monks invited him to spend the night. He agreed on the basis that they supply him with several things. "What is it that you want?" they asked.

"If I spend the night, I must have a pound of butter, a pair of rubber pants, a poker, a cricket bat, and a bass saxophone." It was an unusual request; nevertheless, they scurried around the monastery and found them all. As they went to sleep that night, the monks heard an awesome progression of half tones and squeaks and squawks coming from his room.

The weather continued badly so they asked him to stay another night. He agreed, but only if they again supplied him with a pound of butter, a pair of rubber pants, a poker, a cricket bat, and a bass saxophone. Again, they heard those awful noises emanating from his bedroom. Finally, it was time for him to leave.

The old abbot walked him to the door and said, "We were glad to supply all of those things, but if you don't mind, would you mind telling me why you wanted them?"

The traveler said, "Well, it is a family secret. It's been in my family for years and years. But, if you promise not to tell another living soul, I'll tell you."

So, he told the abbot, and the abbot, being a man of his word, never told another living soul.

We shall never know why or what he did with those things.

When we follow Christ, we are often are forced to live with mystery. If Jesus cannot answer it all, neither can we. We wait in darkness. And one day, by faith, God will give light in the next life. We wait in darkness, And, one day, by faith, God will give light in the next life.

Application Two: Bruised hearts often emit the sweetest fragrances.

My daughters used to raid my rose garden. They cut off my best roses, crushed them, and squeezed them into plastic baggies to make homemade perfume. We need not shake many bushes in our lives before we find dozens of roses soon to be crushed and squeezed to make sweet-smelling perfume.

Application Three: One hour of trial gives more insight into the depths of our spiritual lives than ten years of prosperity.

April said to me, "Life is not measured by the breaths you take, but by the moments that take your breath away."

I don't enjoy troubles. In fact, I don't like them at all. However, I often quote a poem my mother taught me when I was about ten. It helps a lot.

I walked a mile with pleasure,

She chattered all the way,

But left me none the wiser

For all she had to say.

I walked a mile with Sorrow,

And ne'er a word said she,

But, oh, the things I learned from her

When Sorrow walked with me!"

Application Four: Hold everything loosely. God has the right to give and to take away.

Ray Stedman tells of giving a dinner speech at a convention. He forgot his suit. He went to a nearby mortuary and asked to borrow one for the day. That evening he decided to place his notes into the coat pocket of the suit or safe keeping. He couldn't find a pocket. Suddenly, it dawned on him that cadaver suits have no pockets.

One of my dreams was to pastor the same church for 40 years. I started at Casas when I was 25. I was going to retire from being senior pastor at Casas when I reached 65. But that never happened—too much heart damage. I couldn't keep that pace anymore.

Along the way, I learned to hold things loosely. I know that successful hand-off rates from one senior pastor to the next is abysmal. So, with careful planning and laying groundwork for 15 years, I have transitioned the church to younger leadership. I baptized the new Senior Pastor when he was six. I had my fun. Now it's their turn. The church is thriving into the next generation.

I held onto my dream loosely. When God said, "Give it up," I could give it up. God now has other things in store for me.

Application Five: God never promised to remove all sufferings. He did promise to provide the grace and strength we need to live victoriously through them.

Mastering this fifth application means learning contentment. Philippians 4:10-13 was my dad's favorite Bible passage. I, too, use it often:

> *"I rejoice greatly in the Lord that at last you have renewed your concern for me. Indeed, you were concerned, but you had no opportunity to show it. I am not saying this because I am in need, for I have learned to be content whatever the circumstances. I know what it is to be in need, and I know what it is to have plenty. I have learned the secret of being content in any and every situation, whether well fed or hungry, whether living in plenty or in want. I can do all things through him who gives me strength." (NIV)*

My dad was in great shape at 84 when the lymphoma hit. The doctors tried numerous drugs with little success. The last try was an experimental drug. In December I took dad to his doctor for an update on the success or failure of the new drug.

"Well, Roger," the doctor said to dad, "The new drug's not working. We might as well stop using it."

"OK, what are we going to try next?"

The doctor paused, and with what I thought was sincere and genuine empathy, said, "There is no next. There is nothing more we can do. We are out of drugs and ideas."

I watched my dad react as he heard his life was over. What must it be like to be told to go home and die?

"How long do I have?"

"Three months or less."

He bowed his head and shook it softly back and forth: "Well then, I guess this is it."

I rolled him in his wheelchair out into the hall and by the nurses' station we'd passed so many times before. We would never pass that way again.

I wanted to comfort him. But sometimes it is best to keep quiet. After a while he spoke, "Well, Osh (He called me "Osh"—it was my little boy nickname), 'I can do all things through Christ who strengthens me.'"

> *Take a moment now and consider your worldview. Is it a biblical one or of some other variety? Can you see how much of our suffering is viewed as part of the natural course of life and not God's fault?*
>
> *Consider some of your sufferings. Do they make sense in light of your worldview? Think of a trouble you are now enduring. Go through the checklist and see if God gives you insight into what and why you are experiencing what you're going through.*
>
> *Now, consider an even further surrender into God's love and grace. Enjoy His presence for a moment. Then pray again for God to mold you into a spiritual mother or father at any price.*
>
> *Amen.*

CHAPTER 11

THE TEMPLE

Julie and I often pick a Bible subject to study when we have some time off. We were sitting in the car trapped in a construction zone in Pittsburgh and had yet to pick our study topic. Julie asked me, "Have you ever heard a sermon on the difference between the soul and the spirit?"

"No," I replied. "The truth is I have no idea what a soul is, much less a spirit. I've never heard anyone preach or teach about it. I never saw a book on discerning or analyzing the spirit—or the soul. Let's make that our study."

At the bookstore I found a three-volume work by Watchman Nee called, "The Spiritual Man." His book was a guide to understanding the spirit and the soul.[39]

We began with a Bible concordance and categorized many of the verses containing the words, "body," "soul," "spirit" and "heart," What is a spirit? What is man's soul? What is the difference between the Holy Spirit and our human spirit? How does the soul fit into all of this?" What is the meaning and functions of each?

I need for you to bear with me in this chapter. It is a teaching chapter regarding essential foundations for understanding what makes a spiritual mother or father and for understanding the spiritual nature of mankind.

The Greek words are intriguing.

"Spirit" is the Greek word "pneuma" which is translated into English as spirit, breath, or wind. We get words like "pneumatic" from this Greek word.

"Soul" is the Greek word "psyche." From psyche we get words like "psychology."

"Soma"" is the Greek word for body.

Combine soul and body and we get words like "Psychosomatic," which describes those whose minds tell them something is wrong with their bodies when, in fact, there is not.

Dichotomy Or Trichotomy

Some argue man has only two parts. This view describes man as a dichotomy. Those who believe this combine spirit and soul into one entity. Julie and I found it hard to justify this theological position. Paul certainly believed God designed man with three different and distinct parts: a spirit, a soul, and a body. This is called a "trichotomy." Paul was concerned for the sanctifying spiritual growth of all three parts:

> "May God himself, the God of peace, sanctify you through and through. May your whole spirit, soul and body be kept blameless at the coming of our Lord Jesus Christ." 1 Thessalonians 5:23-24 (NIV)

Soon we will see how the Word of God dividing between soul and spirit, and joints and marrow (flesh and bones), enables us to distinguish God's voice from personal or Satanic counterfeits.

> For the word of God is living and active. Sharper than any double-edged sword, it penetrates even to dividing soul and spirit, joints and marrow; it judges the thoughts and attitudes of the heart." Hebrews 4:12-13 (NIV)

The term, "word of God", does not refer solely to the Bible. The Bible had yet to be written. The writer to the Hebrews is identifying Jesus as the "Word" ("logos") of God. This philosophical Greek term describes the "unrevealed wisdom of God". John wrote in John 1:

> "In the beginning was the Word and the Word was with God and the Word was God." John 1:1 (NIV)

In verse 14 he declares that the *"Word became flesh and made his dwelling among us." (NIV)*

By the way, the word, "heart", can be understood as either soul or spirit depending upon on the context in which it's used.

The creation story introduced the terms "spirit" and "soul".

> *"The Lord God formed the man from the dust of the ground and breathed (spirited) into his nostrils the breath (spirit) of life (soul), and man became a living soul" (Genesis 2:7).*

In simple terms, God fashioned a body (soma) out of dirt and then breathed His Spirit (pneuma) into the body (soma). One body plus one spirit equals a living soul (psyche).

When Breath Is Gone

Once upon a time people were assumed dead when they stopped breathing. But today, no one is really sure when the moment of death occurs. Some bodies are brain dead as measured by EEGs, but still breathing. If there's no brain activity, we debate whether it is legal or moral to unplug them from the breathing machines.

Distinguishing between life and death was simpler in biblical times. Moses used the same test I used when my daughter Jessie died. I put my cheek down to her little nostrils to see if I could feel any breath. There was none. I knew she was off to glory.

Translated in English, the Jews used the terms "breath," "wind," and "spirit" interchangeably. If someone was breathing, there was a spirit inside. When the breath stopped, he or she was dead. The spirit had departed.

Through the years some Jewish cultures developed an idea that when the spirit left, it hovered around the body for three days before departing to the place of the dead. The TV series "M*A*S*H" (about a Mobile Army Surgical Hospital working just behind the front lines during the Korean War) used this idea as the core for one particular episode.

An American soldier died in the MASH unit as the doctors struggled to save his life. For three days his spirit hung around the unit. He could see and hear all the living people, but none of the living could see or communicate with him. Finally, after three days, in a strangely sobering scene, he unwillingly joined a long line of soldiers, American, Korean, Chinese, and Russian who were all shuffling off together to the place of the dead.

This illustrates why Jesus waited four days before departing for Bethany to bring Lazarus back to life (John 11). After four days there was absolutely no doubt in anyone's mind that Lazarus was totally dead.

According to Psalm 49, the reason man is separate and distinct from all other animals is because he alone has an eternal spirit. Animals have bodies and souls. But man is different. He has a body, soul, and a spirit.

Oftentimes the Bible refers to men and women as living beings or souls. The term "soul" is used two ways. It is used in a restrictive sense as in body, soul, and spirit. It is also used in a broader sense to refer to the whole being of a man. For example, we read in 1 Peter 3 that eight souls (psyche) went into the ark before the flood commenced.

An Allegory

In 1 Corinthians 6:19 Paul used an allegory to help us better understand the inner spiritual workings of mankind: *"Do you not know that your bodies are temples of the Holy Spirit, who is in you?" (NIV)* Paul never compared the body to the house of the Holy Spirit. Each of us is a temple of the Holy Spirit.

The temple had three parts. First were the outer courts surrounded the temple building itself. Inside, the temple was divided into two main parts. The holy place occupied the front two-thirds of the building. Here the priests ministered daily in worship to God. The holy of holies, which made up the back third of the temple, was behind the curtain separating the two sections. Inside the holy of holies was the ark of the covenant, with the mercy seat under the shadowing wings of two cherubim.

If we were to ask any Israelite in Bible times, "Where does God live?" The answer was simple—and always the same: "He inhabits the universe and He manifests His presence on the mercy seat deep inside the holy of holies."

Most anyone could have access to the courts outside the temple. Only some of the priests could come into the holy place. Only the high priest could go into the holy of holies and then only once a year on the Day of Atonement.

When Paul wrote that the human body is like the temple, he used an allegory to describe the nature of mankind. The following picture summarizes our entire beings. Use it as a reference as I describe each part.

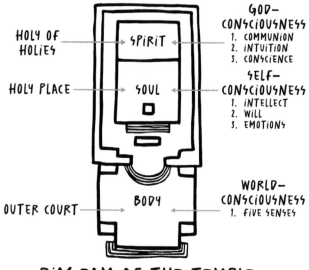

DIAGRAM OF THE TEMPLE

The outer courts correspond to the human body (soma) which is our organ of world consciousness. Our bodies are the outside part of us that utilizes the five senses to put us in touch with the world. We see each other, touch, feel, sense each other, and communicate with each other through our bodies.

Next is the soul (psyche). This part of the temple model corresponds to our holy place which is our organ of self-consciousness. Our souls are the essence of who we are. This is our mind ("nous"), "me," my personality, myself.

The Bible ascribes three functions to the soul. It is the source of our intellect, will, and emotions. Any psychology textbook will describe intellect, will, and emotions as the definition of personhood.

The innermost part of our being is our human spirit (pneuma) which is our organ of God consciousness. When Christ enters our lives at the moment of salvation, He does not come to live in our souls. He comes to live in our human spirits. This is our holy of holies. A study of the Bible verses on spirit reveals that the human spirit also has three main functions. It is the source of our intuition, conscience, and communion with God.

The Ten Commandments were placed in the ark of the covenant inside the holy of holies. God revealed His will and intentions through the law. Today, God reveals His will and intentions in our own holy of holies. It is there he communes and speaks with us.

We find an example of this in Mark 2:8: *"Immediately Jesus knew in His spirit that this was what they were thinking in their hearts." (NIV)*

In the days before Christ, God received worship in the holy of holies. Once a year, the high priest sprinkled blood on the mercy seat to bring forgiveness of sin for the entire nation. At the moment of Christ's resurrection, the curtain hanging in the temple between the holies of holies and the holy place was ripped in two from top to bottom. This means God has opened the way and we now have full access into the throne room of God. We no longer need a priest to approach God on our behalf.

> *"Yet a time is coming and has now come when the true worshipers will worship the Father in spirit and truth, for they are the kind of worshipers the Father seeks. God is spirit and His worshipers must worship in spirit and in truth." John 4:23-24 (NIV)*

More than one thousand years before Christ, the Ten Commandments, which represented the law, were stored inside the ark in the temple. (The ark was lost when the Babylonians conquered Judah and destroyed the temple.) The law accused or excused the Israelites' behaviors. Today our consciences help to define our conduct based on the guidance in our innermost spirit.

Paul illuminated this aspect of the human spirit in Romans 9:1:

> *"I speak the truth in Christ—I am not lying—my conscience confirms it through the Holy Spirit." (NIV)*

Our human spirit is one place deep within us where no one but God is allowed to enter. Just as the average person could not go from the outside courts into the holy place, and just as most of the priests could not go from the holy place into the holy of holies, no one can enter into our innermost spirit except God Himself. Here is where we meet with God, listen to Him, gain guidance, wisdom, and forgiveness. It is here much of our communion and worship really occur.

Because we are Christians, Satan can never enter into our inner human spirits. This is where God dwells. Our inner spirit is protected from Satan. But, Satan can surely attack our souls and bodies. The struggle with Satan is always for control of our minds – our intellect, will, and emotions.

Think in terms of three concentric circles. The outside circle represents our bodies. The next inner circle represents our souls. The innermost circle represents our human spirit. God usually moves from the inside out. Satan usually attacks from the outside in.

Now, let's imagine another model utilizing three interconnecting circles.

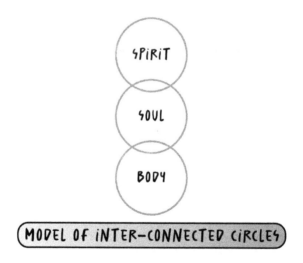

MODEL OF INTER-CONNECTED CIRCLES

What happens in the soul is crucial because the soul is where we make choices. When we choose to follow the promptings and guidance of the indwelling Holy Spirit we live as spiritual men and women.

On the other hand, the soul, the seat of our personhood, can also choose to suppress our spirit and live by our own wants and desires. We are now operating no longer as spiritual but as what Paul describes in 1 Corinthians 2:10-16 as "soul" (psyche) men and women who are without the spirit. It is possible to be indwelt by the Spirit of God and not live like it.

It is only when the soul submits to the promptings of God that the spirit can lead as God designed.

Let's imagine for a moment what living in the spirit or soul or body might look like. I struggle with the sin of gluttony. I know all about diets, since I have tried them all. I know the tendency to be overweight is 70% genetic. I know the number of amino acids, hormones, endocrine secretions, metabolism rates, thyroid problems, and neurotransmitters that combine to produce body size is complex. I know there are enzymes at the top and bottom of our stomachs that tell us when we need to eat more and when to stop.

I also know for most of us, we choose how much to eat. I mean, after all, I have never eaten an accidental bite of food in my life. When food is so plentiful, smells so good, looks so inviting and my body is enticing me, I succumb too often. This is an example of living by the promptings of my body.

My colon disease was debilitating before an ileostomy operation brought things under control. The pain, bleeding, and gastritis made life miserable. I had to resist focusing on my bodily problems to the exclusion of focusing my internal human spirit where God lives. A vast difference exists between focusing on the body and being miserable versus focusing on the spirit and watching God use the experience to make me more like Jesus.

"The Bible says Christians are not to be unequally yoked to non-Christians," I said to the young lady sitting before me. "That means Christians are not to marry non-Christians." Her fiancé was not a Christian and she wanted to know if God would bless their marriage. I explained that marrying a non-Christian is like two people working from a different set of blueprints.

One set is God-designed and the other is not. Unfortunately, the promptings of her soul were too strong for her. Her intellect and emotions were more powerful than the leadership of the Spirit of God within her spirit. By an act of her will, she married him anyway. Two years later she was in my office weeping as she detailed her recent divorce.

Julie was communing with God quietly in prayer. She looked up at me and says, "Brie," our daughter who lives 980 miles away, "is in trouble. Let's pray for her." Moments later her husband called. Brie was in the hospital struggling for her life. She had arrived by ambulance moments earlier. Julie was already packing for the flight to Dallas.

God originally designed Adam with all three parts in perfect balance. Think of Adam as being like a three-story building. The lower floor was his body. The middle floor was his soul. The upper floor was his spirit where God lived.

When Adam and Eve ate the fruit from the Tree of the Knowledge of Good and Evil (Genesis 3:1-6) a spiritual bomb exploded inside Adam's spirit and decimated the third floor. Cracks opened in the second and on down into the first story. Adam was going to die—both physically and spiritually.

The bomb of self-willed disobedience wreaked great havoc on Adam's entire being. Genesis 2:8-17 recorded God's planting of two critical trees in the Garden of Eden: the tree of life and the tree of the knowledge of good and evil. In Genesis 2:16-17 God gave Adam specific instructions regarding the trees:

> *"And the Lord God commanded the man, 'You are free to eat from any tree in the garden; but you must not eat from the tree of the knowledge of good and evil, for when you eat from it, you will certainly die.'" (NIV)*

Let's not miss the spiritual principle. The tree of life represents life in the spirit. The tree of the knowledge of good and evil represents life lived out of the soul.

The real issue in the garden revolved around how Adam and Eve would live. They could choose to live by the promptings of God in their inner human spirit; or they could choose to live by the cravings in their souls. A careful examination of Genesis 3:1-6 reveals that the serpentine attack was aimed directly at Eve's soul:

*Now the serpent was more crafty than any of the wild animals
the Lord God had made. He said to the woman, "Did God
really say, 'You must not eat from any tree in the garden?'"
The woman said to the serpent, "We may eat fruit from the
trees in the garden, but God did say, You must not eat fruit
from the tree that is in the middle of the garden, and you must
not touch it, or you will die." Genesis 3:1-3 (NIV)*

In the attack on Eve's intellect. Satan did not accurately repeat
God's instructions. Eve was vulnerable because she was unable
to correctly repeat God's instructions. God said nothing about
touching the fruit. The struggle between Satan and Eve was for her
soul because her soul is where she will make the choice to follow
God or not. Satan attacked in three areas. He confused her intellect,
appealed to her emotions, and then seduced her will.

No one knows the duration of her temptation experience. The
struggle may have continued for years, for months, or perhaps for
minutes. However, it continued long enough for Satan to get her
confused and to entice her with the look and smell of the fruit. Then,
when Satan convinced her she could be like God, she surrendered
her will and ate the fruit.

*"You will not certainly die," the serpent said to the woman.
"For God knows that when you eat from it, your eyes will be
opened and you will be like God, knowing good and evil."
When the woman saw that the fruit of the tree was good for
food and pleasing to the eye, and also desirable for gaining
wisdom, she took some and ate it. She also gave some to her
husband, who was with her, and he ate it. Genesis 3:4-6 (NIV)*

Perhaps Satan confused Eve but not Adam because Adam
heard God's commands about the trees firsthand. Eve's information
came secondhand as repeated to her by Adam. It may well be that
Satan got to Adam's mind, will, and emotions through his emotional
attachment for Eve.

On the other hand, it may well be that Adam was caught up in
the emotional moment of thinking what it would be like to be like
God. He did not see that in his desire to be like God he was instead
becoming like Satan. Subsequently, Adam surrendered his will, ate
the forbidden fruit and the spiritual bomb exploded.

Satan's goal is always to seize the will. Spiritual battles always occur in the mind or on the body. The battle for the mind is for control of the will. The issue is, "Who will be in charge of my life? Jesus Christ, Satan, or me?"

Jesus will never take control of our minds. He wants us free to choose His way by an act of our own free will. He will never coerce or manipulate us. On the other hand, Satan doesn't hesitate to take control of anything in our lives he can get his hands on.

Whatever in our lives is not under the direct guidance and life of the Holy Spirit is open to control by a demonic spirit *"... and that they will come to their senses and escape from the trap of the devil, who has taken them captive to do his will" (2 Timothy 2:26)*.

As we develop into becoming spiritual young men and women, we need to keep in mind the three classes of Christians. Jessie Penn Lewis in her book *War on The Saints* warns us to keep alert in order to avoid the sneaky deceptions of the Evil One—especially the moment we decide to go on to maturity at any price.

Class One describes Christians who have yet to surrender fully to Christ and who are easily deceived by Satan. Class One Christians are often deceived because they think all things spiritual come from God.

Class Two describes Christians who are maturing into spiritual young women and men. They are surrendered but deceived, still thinking all spiritual things are from God.

Class Three describes Christians who are fully surrendered to Christ and who understand Satan is alive and well and not everything spiritual comes from God.

The most dangerous moment in the life of a Christian may well be the moment he or she decides to go on to maturity at any price— to move from Category One to Category Two. It is guaranteed that Satan will offer a counterfeit at that moment. He offered a counterfeit to Adam and Eve in the garden; he will offer one to us, too.

"Do you want to be like Jesus?" Satan asks.

"Yes, that is the desire of my heart! I want to be like Jesus."

Be careful. Sometimes we start out to look like Jesus and end up looking like Satan—because of spiritual pride.

Counterfeits are not all alike—because we are not all alike—but their purpose is the same. They are intended to seduce us into a kind of life that is not the abundant life at all.

The explosion during Adam's and Eve's headlong fall into sin distorted God's balanced design horribly out of proportion. Let's use our model of three interlocking circles to understand a simple schematic of fallen mankind.

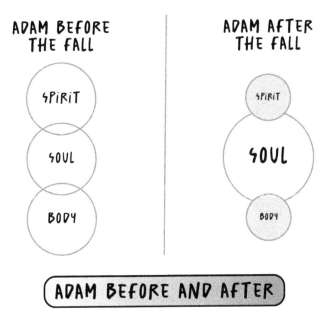

ADAM BEFORE AND AFTER

When they ate the forbidden fruit, Adam's and Eve's intellects soared. After all, they ate from the tree of the knowledge of good and evil. When their knowledge increased, "they became like God, knowing good and evil."

Since the soul is our organ for knowledge or intellect, the size of the human soul swelled into a dominate state never intended by God. The body shriveled and would die. The spirit shriveled and was "darkened." The spirit was no longer God-responsive. It was unable to hear the voice of God (1 Corinthians 2:14). Fallen mankind is far removed from the time when God said, "Let us make mankind in our image."

Fortunately, God provided a plan through Jesus Christ for rebuilding the human spirit so mankind can once again commune with God and live forever. The process of salvation makes the spirit of man alive toward God and to spiritual things. The gospels make clear Jesus suffered to redeem all three parts of us: body, soul, and spirit.

Matthew 26:67 recorded the sufferings of His body:

"Then they spit in his face and struck him with their fists. Others slapped him." (NIV)

Matthew 26:38 documented the suffering of His soul:

"Then he said to them, 'My soul is overwhelmed with sorrow to the point of death.'" (NIV)

Finally, Matthew 27:46 detailed the separation from His Father in his inner spirit:

"Jesus cried out in a loud voice, 'Eli, Eli, lema sabachthani?'— which means, 'My God, my God, why have you forsaken me?'" (NIV)

Since Christ died in body, soul, and spirit, the door to cleansing and restoration swings wide open. The salvation experience continues with the Holy Spirit's work of regeneration. Regeneration (making something alive again) brings life to the spiritually dead human spirit.

Jesus explained to Nicodemus in John 3 how the Holy Spirit gives birth to the human spirit:

"Very truly I tell you, no one can see the kingdom of God unless they are born again."

"How can someone be born when they are old?" Nicodemus asked. "Surely they cannot enter a second time into their mother's womb to be born!"

Jesus answered, "Very truly I tell you, no one can enter the kingdom of God unless they are born of water and the Spirit. Flesh gives birth to flesh, but the Spirit gives birth to spirit. You should not be surprised at my saying, 'You must be born again.' The wind blows wherever it pleases. You hear its sound, but you cannot tell where it comes from or where it is going. So it is with everyone born of the Spirit." John 3:3-8 (NIV)

Let's use the three interlocking circles to imagine how God intends for spiritual growth to progress.

In our early years we were fortunate if our parents were godly Christians who were deeply concerned with our spiritual development. As they taught us to pray, exposed us to Christian fellowship, explained the Bible and took us to relevant, Holy Spirit-anointed churches, they persistently enhanced our spiritual development.

Notice in the diagram below how the soul and spirit mature at both a constant and balanced rate. Neither is dominating the other. Note how the body grows until the age of 20 or so and then hopefully maintains that same size (or close to it) during the following decades. We see here the development of a solidly growing spiritual man or woman.

Our interlocking-circle model demonstrates how God intends for spiritual growth to proceed. Body, soul, and spirit develop in balance and mature right along with each other.

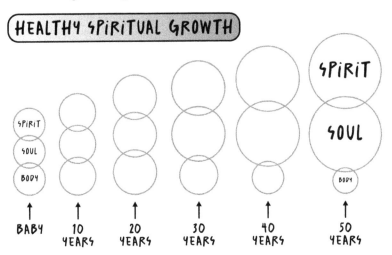

Unfortunately, not all Christians grow according to God's plan. My observation is that as most Christians age, their human spirits shrivel under the domination of an over-developed soul. Like the insidious choice in Genesis, many Christians still choose the tree of knowledge over the tree of the spirit of life.

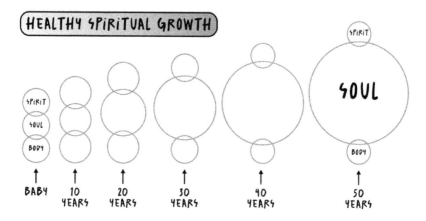

We have here a schematic of what Paul often identified as a carnal, fleshly, or worldly Christian. Worldly Christians are dominated by their souls and inundated by themselves. Notice how spirit, soul, and body begin in balanced proportion. Soon after receiving Christ, the soul grows dramatically in knowledge during the school-age years; but, unfortunately, there is not a corresponding spiritual development.

Soulish desires crowd out spiritual ones. Mental smartness outstrips spiritual acuity. Personal experience and accumulated knowledge are more attractive than godly wisdom. Worldly Christians are so used to following their own wishes and desires that the voice of God is increasingly muffled.

Carnal Christians in their fifties, sixties, and seventies have less spiritual insight than some 16-year-olds. Too many churches are led by men and women who are much more likely to lead out of their souls than out of the inner promptings of God's Holy Spirit.

Some of the most attractive Christians I know are in their senior years and filled with enormous souls of great knowledge and wise experiences—guided by equally well cultivated, well developed, and mature human spirits.

Please understand; knowledge, education, and experience are essential. Paul encouraged Timothy to study hard as he prepared for the ministry. I love to study and learn. I deeply appreciate the solid educational foundation I received both as a child and as an adult. I am just saying that as we go about the work of increasing our knowledge and intellect, we must have a corresponding increase in our innermost spirit. We never want to be in a position where our spirits are less important than our souls.

I wonder sometimes if too much emphasis is placed in Bible colleges and seminaries on books and learning and not enough on maturing, cultivating, and utilizing the innermost human spirit where God dwells.

Now, take a moment as we conclude this lesson and consider what your three-interlocking circles look like. Have you waxed strong in soul—to the neglect and detriment of your spirit? Are you a spiritual man or woman in good spiritual balance? Is your soul in humble submission to your spirit? Or is it grotesquely misshapen and grown out of proportion to your human spirit? Do you live by the promptings of your soul or of your spirit?

The real question is: "We will we live by the spirit or by the soul?" The drama of Adam and Eve is acted out every day in our lives. Which tree will we choose?

Dear Lord Jesus,

Help me overcome the driving voices of soul and body which too often assault me. Help me listen carefully to the promptings of the Holy Spirit. My desire is to live by the Spirit and not by the soul or body. I want to hear you speak in my inner spirit so I can choose you and your will for my life. Mature me into a spiritual mother or father at any price

Amen.

CHAPTER 12

CULTIVATION

Spiritual maturity must be carefully cultivated.

The human spirit must mature since it does not come ready to operate. At the time of conversion, the spirit is cold, darkened, and shrunken. At the moment of conversion, it awakens. It's like the light turns on and we begin to grow spiritually. But it does not blossom immediately.

Think about Jesus' early growth as Luke recorded in Luke 2:40: *"And the child grew and became strong; he was filled with wisdom, and the grace of God was on him." (NIV)* He was not born spouting spiritual truth. He could not even add two plus two and get four.

As fully human He had to learn and mature just like we do. Joseph and Mary obviously helped Him understand His mission on earth. Can you imagine Mary putting the child Jesus on her knee and reading Psalm 22 (the Psalm of the cross) which contains verses like: "My God, My God, why have you forsaken me? ... They pierce my hands and feet ... I thirst (literally "My mouth is dried up") ... They cast lots for my garments ... It is finished! (literally "He has done it!")." (NIV)

Mary whispered, "Jesus, this is all about you."

The early years of John the Baptist are described in Luke 1:80 as years of maturing his inner human spirit: *"And the child grew and became strong in spirit; and he lived in the wilderness until he appeared publicly to Israel." (NIV)*

If Jesus and John the Baptist needed to cultivate their innermost human spirit, so will we.

"Therefore, I urge you, brothers and sisters, in view of God's mercy, to offer your bodies as a living sacrifice, holy and pleasing to God—this is your true and proper worship. Do not conform to the pattern of this world, but be transformed by the renewing of your mind. Then you will be able to test and approve what God's will is—his good, pleasing and perfect will." Romans 12:1-2 (NIV)

Praying In the Spirit As Well As In the Mind

Praying in the spirit as well as in the mind (or soul) is essential for developing a strong prayer life.

"For if I pray in a tongue, my spirit prays, but my mind is unfruitful. So what shall I do? I will pray with my spirit, but I will also pray with my understanding; I will sing with my spirit, but I will also sing with my understanding." 1 Corinthians 14:14-15 (NIV)

When I think of praying in my mind (my soul) I think of using a prayer list. I have people and things I pray for every day. Often I have a list in hand. I will use the ACTS acrostic to guide my prayers: Adoration, Confession, Thanksgiving, and Supplication (requests). These prayers come from my soul. On the other hand, praying in my spirit leads me into the presence of God. Here, I listen for Him to speak Holy Spirit to human spirit. Here I pray for people and things and issues as God reveals them to me.

Sometimes, I use the word "knower" to describe communing and communicating with God in my human spirit. It is like sensing God speaking to me down deep in my "knower," The more intimate we are with Christ, the easier it is to identify the voice of God deep within our human spirit. Jesus said, "My sheep know my voice."

The gatekeeper opens the gate for him, and the sheep listen to his voice. He calls his own sheep by name and leads them out. When he has brought out all his own, he goes on ahead of them, and his sheep follow him because they know his voice." John 10:3-4 (NIV)

During a class in seminary, the evangelism professor caught my attention when he said, "You men had best not stay in Texas when you graduate. Texas has more than enough preachers."

Shortly after graduating from seminary, my wife, Julie, and I prayed for an opportunity to pastor in a place with many non-Christians and not many churches. Since there were more than 40 churches within a three-mile radius of my own home church in Dallas, we sensed we were needed elsewhere.

One Sunday afternoon the phone rang as I prepared to go to Denver to meet with a church to consider being their pastor.

The caller was from Tucson. "We have your resumé. Could you interview with our church next week?" We talked for several minutes until I had to excuse myself. I had to catch the plane to Denver.

While talking with Doris from Tucson, I felt God telling me I would become pastor of the Tucson church. I hung up the phone and turned to Julie: "I'm going to go to Denver; but God just told me we are going to pastor in Tucson."

Julie's smiled, "I know. While you were talking, He told me the same thing."

By the way, a heavy snow was falling when I arrived in Denver. The deacon who picked me up at the airport slipped on the ice and cursed as he dropped my suitcase. I took this as a sign from God I wasn't going to pastor in Denver. (And Denver is one of my favorite cities in the entire world!)!

A week later Julie and I were on the airplane to Tucson. We have pastored that same church for over 40 years now with never a doubt that Tucson was the place God called us to minister.

People sometimes ask, "How did you know for sure you would pastor in Tucson?"

I don't try to explain all about the human soul and spirit. I usually ask them, "Have you ever had that experience when deep down inside you just know what to do? When it seems God Himself gives you impressions, encouragement, advice, and peace that you are on the right track? What you are sensing is the Holy Spirit speaking to you, Holy Spirit to human spirit!"

This is where I often use the descriptive term, "knower." My "knower" is my human spirit.

Most Christians indicate they have had similar experiences of sensing the promptings of the Spirit deep within. They just didn't know what to call it.

I have a three-point checklist I use before every sermon. First, I check that my microphone is turned on. Second, I pray the Holy Spirit will enable me communicate spirit to spirit with the folks that day. Finally, I check that my zipper is closed, and then I walk to the pulpit to preach.

One of the first things I do to cultivate my spirit is to quiet down my mind. We live in a society of frantic activity. God has a hard time speaking to busy people who never take time to sit and be still. Frantic activity, racing thoughts, and media bombardment demand our energy and attention. God says: *"Be still and know that I am God." Psalm 46:10 (NIV)*

There comes a time for ceasing from the frenzy of daily activity to rest in the presence of the Lord. It is only then we will hear the "gentle whisper" of the still small voice of God. The whirlwind blew by Elijah, but God was not in the wind. The earth shook, but God was not in the quaking. Thunder and lightning flashed and roared, but God was not in the storm. Then, when all was still and quiet, God spoke to Elijah (see 1 Kings 19:11-13).

Current American society encourages us to oscillate between frenzy and collapse. The principle of listening quietly to the promptings of the Spirit is a lost art in our media-saturated culture teeming with radio waves, television waves, computers, the internet, smartphones, Xboxes, and social media, just to name a few thieves of quietness and peace.

Taking every thought captive (2 Corinthians 10:5) begins the critical path that leads to the proper mental, spiritual, and emotional state for hearing from God. Try to sit quietly and refuse to let your mind run away in uncontrolled thinking for five minutes. Most can't do it. When your mind wanders into today's upcoming activities, or yesterday's failures, stop it! Don't go there. Instead, stay in the present and anticipate the upcoming moments communing with God.

I like to meditate on favorite Scripture passages to keep my mind from wandering. For example, I like to imagine I am on my hands and knees looking up at the Shepherd in Psalm 23. The Lord looks so tall and rugged and gentle. I picture Him picking me up in his arms and hugging me. The sense of peace and security is incredible.

Once upon a time, I felt like all hell was breaking loose around me. I remember getting quiet before God and thinking about the last

Israelite in line when Moses led the people through the Red Sea. What would it be like to see the Egyptian armies coming up rapidly from the rear and wondering whether I would reach the other side in time?

I see Moses far ahead with the rod of God lifted high. I am hurrying. I am embarrassed to run past the women and children, so I hang back to help them along all the while keeping an eye out behind on the rapidly closing chariots. It seems like I will get to Moses none too soon—maybe not soon enough. Then, finally, I pass Moses as the rod descends. The waters close cataclysmically. I am safe.

This Red Sea meditation of deliverance has remained with me for years. When the enemy armies surround me, Jesus stands with arms outstretched. At that moment, I am mentally and spiritually prepared to meet in my human spirit with God the Holy Spirit.

I love to meditate upon David's Psalm 131.

> *"O Lord, my heart is not lifted up, my eyes are not raised too high; I do not occupy myself with things too great and too marvelous for me. But I have calmed and quieted my soul, like a child quieted at his mother's breast; like a child that is quieted is my soul. O Israel, hope in the Lord from this time forth and forevermore." (RSV)*

Practice quieting your mind. Don't allow it to wander. Keep your mind focused. Be still and take every thought captive. Meditate on a Bible verse or passage that draws you into the heart of God. A quiet mind is the foundation for special times in your spiritual throne room deep within.

A godly person, the Bible says, is like a tree planted by streams of water (Psalm 1). Trees are not frenzied or frantic. They do not consume vast amounts of caffeine to keep adrenaline flowing. Trees are unhurried. They do not wander from their source. They quietly produce fruit.

God never reveals the deep things of the spirit to the Christian who just drops by for a little chat.

Keeping The Temporal and Eternal In Perspective

The art of spiritual maturity is learning to transition from the temporal to the eternal. Our human nature leads us most naturally to focus on the temporary things of earth like material possessions, human relationships, physical health, and so forth. On the other hand, our spiritual nature has an eternal focus in mind.

The weeping woman beside me at the casket was disconsolate. Her best friend's four-year-old son drowned after riding his tricycle into a swimming pool. "Why?" she pleaded. "Why did this have to happen? Where was his guardian angel? Why didn't God prompt some adult to walk out just in time to stop him?

She was hurting, so I first took some time to comfort her. But that was not enough to calm her raging heart. She wanted some sort of answer to make some sort of sense to this tragedy. At what seemed like the right moment I quietly asked her, "What is God's ultimate plan for believers?"

"To be with Jesus," she replied.

"Where is that little boy?"

"With Jesus!"

We will never sustain an eternal prayer life unless we determine to develop an eternal perspective. We must never allow temporal discomforts to destroy our view of God as He proceeds with His sanctifying and maturing work.

Amid difficult times our humanity cries out, "God heal my body," or "God fix these circumstances," or perhaps, "God turn around this tragedy." However, sometimes God whispers 2 Corinthians 4:16-18:

> *"Therefore we do not lose heart. Though outwardly we are wasting away, yet inwardly we are being renewed day by day. For our light and momentary troubles are achieving for us an eternal glory that far outweighs them all. So we fix our eyes not on what is seen, but on what is unseen, since what is seen is temporary, but what is unseen is eternal." (NIV)*

Transitioning from the temporal to the eternal is accomplished by learning to pray from the inside out.[41] Let's use our three concentric circle model. Remember the human spirit is the innermost circle. The next outer circle represents the soul (the psyche, the mind, the place where I myself live) and the outer circle is the body.

Paul's prayers reveal his deep concern for the maturing of the internal-eternal human spirit. He seldom prayed for anyone's body to get well—he never stopped praying for the development of the inner person. Here are two examples:

For this reason, ever since I heard about your faith in the Lord Jesus and your love for all God's people, I have not stopped giving thanks for you, remembering you in my prayers. I keep asking that the God of our Lord Jesus Christ, the glorious Father, may give you the Spirit of wisdom and revelation, so that you may know him better. I pray that the eyes of your heart may be enlightened in order that you may know the hope to which he has called you, the riches of his glorious inheritance in his holy people, and his incomparably great power for us who believe. Ephesians 1:15-19 (NIV)

For this reason I kneel before the Father, from whom every family in heaven and on earth derives its name. I pray that out of his glorious riches he may strengthen you with power through his Spirit in your inner being, so that Christ may dwell in your hearts through faith. And I pray that you, being rooted and established in love, may have power, together with all the Lord's holy people, to grasp how wide and long and high and deep is the love of Christ, and to know this love that surpasses knowledge —that you may be filled to the measure of all the fullness of God. Ephesians 3:14-19 (NIV)

Putting your name or one of your friends or loved one's name in those verses will bless your heart —and theirs. Only one of Paul's recorded prayers show him praying for the healing of someone's bodily infirmity. Three times he prayed for his "thorn" to be removed; but, after Jesus said no, he accepted his thorn as part of God's plan and stopped praying for healing. I am certain he prayed for others to be healed; however, those requests are most likely not recorded because they were so insignificant compared to his prayers for maturing the inner spirits of his readers.

For example, when Timothy was sick with various stomach ailments Paul did not pray for his healing. Neither did he send him to the local faith healer. He advised him that a little wine would be good for his stomach (1 Timothy 5:23).

God often allows or creates circumstances so we may know Him better. He wants to sensitize our God-consciousness. Satan wants to focus our minds on our bodies or on our circumstances in order to desensitize our God-consciousness. Too often we are obsessed with removing pain and problems. God, on the other hand, is obsessed with divinely sensitizing our inner spirits. Our bodies are temporal and decaying. God will sacrifice the temporal body every time if that is what it takes to mature the eternal.

We can pray multiple times to be healed of cancer; nevertheless, we will eventually succumb to death. Praying for healing is not eternally effective. Life is a terminal disease. There are no Bible verses that describe angels rejoicing when bodies are healed. On the other hand, the angels rejoice when lost sheep enter into eternal life.

> *For we know that if the earthly tent we live in is destroyed, we have a building from God, an eternal house in heaven, not built by human hands. Meanwhile we groan, longing to be clothed instead with our heavenly dwelling. ... Therefore we are always confident and know that as long as we are at home in the body we are away from the Lord. For we live by faith, not by sight. We are confident, I say, and would prefer to be away from the body and at home with the Lord. 2 Corinthians 5:1-8 (NIV)*

Too many Christians beg for God to change their situations and heal their bodies while not having the slightest idea of God's eternal intentions. Praying from the inside out allows us to see things from God's perspective and interpret the circumstances surrounding our lives in light of how our requests affect our inner spirits.

Three Times Is Enough

I think we should follow Paul's example when we pray for healing. Three times is enough. If we aren't healed after three prayers, we can assume God has other things in mind. Let's start praying for wisdom to understand His intentions and get with His plan.

Take a careful look at Paul's own physical healing journey in 2 Corinthians 12:7-9:

> *To keep me from becoming conceited, I was given a thorn in my flesh, a messenger of Satan, to torment me. Three times I pleaded with the Lord to take it away from me. But he said to me, "My grace is sufficient for you, for my power is made perfect in weakness." (NIV)*

While God did not give Paul the healing he wanted, He did give him the grace to handle his situation with success.

"Thorn" is the Greek word describing a "tent stake" driven into the ground to stabilize and secure a tent. The Babylonians used the word to describe sharpened trees used for impaling people. "Torment" is a Greek boxing term meaning, "to beat, to strike with the fist." Paul had a stake impaled in his body, tormenting him to keep him humble.

There are four main guesses as to the nature of Paul's thorn.

First, he was ugly—probably a result of his five beatings with rods, three whippings, and one stoning (2 Corinthians 10:10).

Second, he may have been incapacitated with malaria contracted in the marshy areas of the southern coast of Turkey.

Third, he could have struggled with epilepsy, which was considered in the ancient world to be caused by demons (Galatians 4:3-14).

Finally, and most probable, he had some sort of debilitating eye trouble. Think about the blind scales falling from his eyes at his bright-light conversion in the desert (Galatians 4:15; 6:11; and Acts 22). As he finished the letter to the Galatians Paul took the pen from his amanuensis and wrote a greeting with his own hand. The implication here is that he couldn't see well enough to write an entire letter on his own.

> "See what large letters I use as I write to you with my own hand!" Galatians 6:11 (NIV)

To one degree or other, we are all like Paul in our weaknesses. Pray three times for healing and if the answer is no, then consider that God wants you to live with your sickness and find grace and strength to handle it accordingly.

I was invited to a healing service for an American missionary serving in a Middle Eastern country. People had prayed for his healing for over ten years. Now, it was our turn. I am not a physician, but when we prayed it became increasingly obvious to me that he was struggling with brain-chemistry imbalances (like depression).

When the prayer time ended, I gently told him it was time to stop praying for healing: "If God hasn't healed you after ten years of praying, then another year will probably not do it either. God's answer is, 'Stop asking me for healing. My grace is sufficient for you.'"

I continued, "You get to ask three times, maybe four. Then, it is time to stop praying and figure out how to live for God's glory while the 'thorn' twists in your body."

After the meeting we discussed the genetic implications of his disorder. We shook his family tree and all sorts of ancestors with the same malady fell out. "I believe there is medical treatment available that can give you great relief," I said. "Go see the right doctor."

The next morning the missionary came by the table where I was eating breakfast and said, "Thanks, I needed those insights about Paul and his thorn. I'd forgotten His grace is sufficient."

By the way, praying without considering eternal perspectives can be dangerous. If you pray without being enlightened, without knowing His will, God will sometimes give you what you request with devastating results.

Let me illustrate. Tired of waiting for God's provision, the Israelites in the wilderness began to murmur and complain about God's seeming lack of care. They prayed for meat to eat. They were sick of the manna. So, God answered their prayers by providing diseased quail for them to eat. They soon wished they had never complained. The Bible says that 35,000 died!

> *But they soon forgot what he had done,*
> *and did not wait for his plan to unfold.*
>
> *In the desert they gave in to their craving;*
> *in the wilderness they put God to the test.*
>
> *So he gave them what they asked for,*
> *but sent a wasting disease among them." Psalm 106:13-15 (NIV)*

An awareness of God's will is essential in intelligent praying. Dr. L. Taylor Daniel told a story about a pastor who received a late night call from a mother whose baby was dying. This was long before medical facilities were easily available as they are today. She pleaded with the pastor to pray for her baby to be healed. He replied, "First, let's get on our knees and see how God wants us to pray."

"No, I want to pray for healing now," she demanded.

"I would be glad to pray for your baby; but, first let's kneel and try to get God's insight."

"No," she screamed, "If you won't pray for God to heal my baby, then I will." So, she did. The pastor opened the door and left.

Eighteen years later she watched her son mount the stairs of the village gallows to be hanged for murdering the family of six next door. [42]

Making Intimacy with God a Priority

Quality time and consistent effort lay the foundation for a close relationship with God (or anyone else for that matter). Therefore, to spend more time with his Father, Jesus often withdrew alone to pray.

> *When Jesus heard what had happened, he withdrew by boat privately to a solitary place. Matthew 14:13a (NIV)*
>
> *Very early in the morning, while it was still dark, Jesus got up, left the house and went off to a solitary place, where he prayed. Mark 1:35 (NIV)*
>
> *One of those days Jesus went out to a mountainside to pray, and spent the night praying to God. Luke 6:12 (NIV)*

In Exodus 33:9-11 God met with Moses face to face. In Genesis 3:8, we learn Adam had been intimate with God in the Garden. In Genesis 5:23-24 Enoch was so close with God that God took him to heaven. James 2:23 tells us Abraham was God's friend.

Jeanne Guyon reminds us of Christ's lovely invitation:

> *All who are thirsty, come.*
>
> *All who are starving, come.*
>
> *You who are poor, come.*
>
> *You who are afflicted, come.*
>
> *You who are weighted down with a load of pain, come and be comforted.*
>
> *You who are sick and need a physician, come.*
>
> *You may think you are simple or uneducated or inexperienced in the ways of the Lord or you are very far from a deep experience from the Lord. If that is your case, the Lord has especially chosen you. You are the one most suited to know Him well.* [43]

The Lord searches for men and women who will commune with Him. What does it do to your heart to hear His pleading in the opening pages of the Book of Revelation for lost sheep to come to Him and be saved? What does it do to your heart that Jesus wants to come into our lives and share fellowship with us? He would never force Himself into our lives. He is waiting for us to open the door so He might enter.

> Here I am! I stand at the door and knock. If anyone hears my voice and opens the door, I will come in and eat with that person, and they with me. Revelation 3:20 (NIV)

Throwing Up in Church

Not too many people have had the privilege of throwing up during a church service like I had when I was seven. I spent most of the afternoon and early evening eating peanut butter out of the jar with a spoon. When Dad announced, "Time to go to church," I was feeling rather rumbly. We took our seats in the second row. Several minutes into the sermon I felt the peanut butter on the way up and told my mom so. She said, "Just sit still and it will all go away." I couldn't and it didn't.

I have several seemingly simultaneous memories. First, I remember looking at the pastor as he announced to the congregation that a little boy in front was having some problems and that it was all under control and that they didn't need to look and that they would go on with the service. I never heard anyone communicate so much information in so little time.

Second, I remember my mother scooting away from the onslaught as she said, "Oh, so that's where all the peanut butter went." Third, I remember the strong arms of Dick Dickens picking me up from behind as he said, "I'll take care of him." Fourth, I remember the astonishment of being cleaned up by a man I hardly knew—and I wasn't even his son. Fifth, I remember my mother bringing a mop into the bathroom to clean up. Mr. Dickens said to mom, "You take him while I clean up." Six years later, Mr. Dickens donated a pint of his blood for my open-heart surgery.

I also remember two types of people; those who didn't want to look at the peanut butter, smell the smell, or get touched by the onslaught. They scooted away. Some people were like the pastor: "Don't look! The little boy had an accident. Let's not let him be a distraction. We will keep on with the service." These people saw me as a problem.

Mr. Dickens was the other type. He saw a little boy in need, ignored the pastor, and gently carried me to the bathroom, and cleaned up my mess. He saw a person to be cared for and not a problem to be avoided. He exercised several disciplines on my behalf—disciplines like community, fellowship, service, simplicity, and submission.

How we see people affects our levels of compassion and determines how willing we are to draw near to care for those who've have made a mess of their lives. The spiritual disciplines produce the maturity to see the needs and pains of others—and do something about it.

Take a moment and think of some of the spiritual disciplines you've used. Imagine yourself growing big spiritual muscles as you utilize the disciplines for both your own benefit as well as for the benefits of others. Choose one or two you've never experienced and decide right now to practice them this next week. Remember the disciplines are designed to increase our God dependence while decreasing our self-dependence.

Dear Father,

I grant you the freedom to use whatever you consider necessary to mature me to be a spiritual mother/father.

Amen

CHAPTER 13

PURE HEART

Pure hearts see and hear from God.

"Blessed are the pure in heart, for they will see God." Matthew 5:8 (NIV)

However, what if our spirits are not pure? What if our spirits are dirty with sin or self? Whether God's able to speak clearly in our inner spirits depends upon whether our spirits are pure.

The Psalmist surely had this truth in mind when he wrote Psalm 66:18-19.

"If I had cherished sin in my heart, the Lord would not have listened; but God has surely listened and has heard my prayer." (NIV)

A dirty human spirit impairs our ability to hear God speak.

When was the last time you heard God speak? Many folks would say, "It's been a long time." Some people might even say, "I'm not sure I've ever heard God speak."

One brisk and humid October Friday evening our church invited the whole town of Penelope, Texas, to go with us to the skating rink. As we left, the night air was cool and the hot and sweaty bodies of the children made conditions just right for condensation to quickly fog over the car windows.

As pastor I led the procession of church members' back toward home. In my car were eight young grade-school-aged children.

Three blocks after we departed the skating rink, I noticed blinking red lights in my rear-view mirror. The officer behind me was urging me to pull off to the road.

"Why did you run that stop sign?"

"Stop sign? I didn't see a stop sign." I peered back into the gloom, and sure enough, about a block back was a four-way stop sign. I said, "Oh, officer, I just didn't see it."

He said, "Maybe the reason you didn't see it was because you don't have your lights on."

"Don't have my lights on?" Sure enough, I reached inside and pulled on the light switch.

Then, he said, "Maybe the reason you didn't notice that your lights were off was because of all the commotion these children were making which distracted you! Maybe you couldn't see out because your windows are fogged over." Then he said, "Do you realize that the legal maximum number of occupants in a car in Texas is eight? I'm counting nine in your car."

Then the officer said, "I've got enough on you to throw you into the Hillsboro County Jail tonight. Now, you clean off those windows, get those kids quiet, and get out of my town. If I find you in Hillsboro again tonight, I'm going to run you straight into jail."

I got back in the car and yelled, "You kids all shut up!" I got a shirt out of the trunk, and wiped off the windows, turned my lights on, and drove directly out of town.

Now, let's put this story in spiritual terms. Can you imagine that it's possible for our human spirits to be so sinful, impure, and dirty that we cannot hear God speaking to us?

You can imagine that other things besides sin can intrude into our spirits— like jealousy, greed, lust, gluttony, and pride.

However, sins are not the only things that can diffuse our ability to see and hear God. Let's put in some good things into our spirits like jobs, parenting, golf, sports, crocheting, TV watching, wine tasting, bowling, and parties. We look at the diagram and exclaim, "I can't see God anymore. All that stuff is fogging up the holy of holies in my inner spirit!"

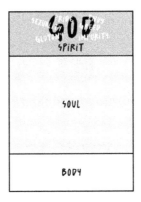

The Bible gives clear warning about the two areas most likely to dirty up a clean spirit: self and sin. In other words: Don't self and don't sin.

Don't Self

"Don't self" is about choosing our own way instead of God's way.

"Do not quench the Spirit." 1 Thessalonians 5:19 (NIV)

How do we quench the Spirit? By refusing or neglecting to follow his leading. Unused, or clogged up, our human spirits shrivel and darken.

On the other hand, when we do what He says, our spirits are exercised. They grow stronger and mature.

For many years Julie and I opened our home every Saturday night and invited our church parishioners to come meet with us for prayer. Attendance averaged about 25. We'd get down on our knees and start praying about the church, the Lord's work, people in need, and the services the next day.

One Saturday night while we were on our knees, I had a deep impression God was saying to me, "Roger, tomorrow morning I don't want you to preach your usual sermon. I want you to walk to the microphone and say simply, 'It is not possible to have fellowship with God while hanging onto all of our sin.' Then walk off the stage."

"Now that was a funny little thought," I said to myself and promptly dismissed it. However, ten minutes later, as I was seeking God in prayer, there again arose this overpowering impression from deep within, "Roger, in the morning, don't preach your prepared sermon."

I replied, "But, God, I've already got it ready to preach! It's a good sermon."

God said, "No, I don't want you to preach that in the morning. He again repeated His instructions.

I was shaken. When the prayer meeting was over, I told Julie what I thought God was saying.

She replied, "You're not really going to do that, are you?"

"I don't know."

The next morning when the alarm went off Julie's first words were, "You're not really going to do that, are you?"

"I don't know. I just don't know."

When I gathered with my ministerial staff early Sunday morning for our prayer time, I thought, "I'll tell these folks what I intend to do. That way it won't be a total shock."

I sensed God say to me, "No, Roger. You may tell no one."

I was dying inside. When the worship time concluded it was now time to preach. I walked to the pulpit, and said, "It is not possible to have fellowship with God while hanging onto all of our sin." and walked off the stage.

Our worship leader asked as I passed by him on the platform, "Where are you going?"

God said to me, "You can't say a word."

I walked off the stage, down the stairs, out the side door, around the church building, went to my office, opened the door, went inside, closed the door, fell on my knees, and wept. "Oh God, oh God, how could you do this to me?" I was so embarrassed—and humiliated.

Later I discovered it was pandemonium in the worship center. Some were saying, "What happened? Did he retire?" Others guessed, "No, I think he had a nervous breakdown." They had no idea what to think. Finally, our worship leader led a couple of songs and dismissed the crowd.

At that time, we offered three identical Sunday morning worship services. I had to repeat my performance twice more. By the third service the word was out. Everyone present for the final service knew what I would do. They came anyway. I did my duty. I did what I sensed God telling me to do.

My family, friends, and congregation know it as my "one-sentence sermon." I would like to relate that thousands of people came to know Christ as a result of that sermon. That didn't happen. I don't know if a single soul was saved. I wish I received hundreds of letters and calls from folks whose lives were changed. No. I did not receive a single one.

In fact, no one said a word to me. Nobody ever mentioned it. It was as if the one-sentence sermon had never occurred. However, I know that while no one ever mentioned it to me, not one soul in attendance that day has forgotten it.

Several months later it began to dawn on me that the sermon was not necessarily for the church. It was for me. I was praying to be a spiritual father at any price. I was praying often to hear God speak, and I think God took me up on the offer. I do know this: my spirit grew and matured dramatically through that weekend. When He speaks, I want to do what he says.

So, practice, don't self. Don't let your self—your self-reliance, self-centeredness, or self-condemnation quench the guidance of the Holy Spirit. Jesus said to His Father, "Not my will, but yours be done." Luke 22:42 (NIV)

Don't Sin

Sin dirties up our spirits and compromises our abilities to see and hear from God. Paul warned in Ephesians 4:30:

> *"And do not grieve the Holy Spirit of God, with whom you were sealed for the day of redemption." (NIV)*

How do we grieve the Holy Spirit? By sinning. Sin grieves Him. It breaks His heart, He weeps over it.

Confession Cleans Up a Dirty Spirit

Confession is God's method for cleansing a dirty spirit. The cleansing process is described in 1 John 1:9:

> *"If we confess our sins, He is faithful and just and will forgive us our sins and purify us from all unrighteousness." (NIV)*

When's the last time you confessed your sins?

When I left for college, my mother sewed a canvas duffle bag and said, "Now here's how you do your laundry." I had never done my laundry. I had other chores growing up, like taking out the trash, washing the dishes, mowing the grass, and making my bed. Mom always did the laundry.

She gave me explicit instructions on how to put my dirty clothes in the bag, find an empty washing machine, put my clothes in the washer, place the coins in the slot, toss in a little detergent and start the machine. This was not hard.

At the end of my first week, I went down the street to a laundromat and found an empty washing machine. Thinking to save a little time, I tossed the duffle bag of dirty clothes into the washer, put in a couple of quarters, and turned on the machine. It spun for only seconds before I heard this ominous, "thunk-thunk-thunk," as my machine began jiggling across the floor. I looked around and saw no one else's washer was jumping and jiggling like mine. It was totally out of balance.

Fortunately, a kind co-ed walked over and reached in front of me while saying, "May I help you?" She opened the lid of my washer and said, "Here, let's empty your clothes out from the bag and then put each of them in the washer. Your clothes will get a lot cleaner. Dirty clothes need individual attention."

Such is the ignorance and naiveté of a college freshman male. I was humiliated.

Every night across Christendom, many Christians say bedtime prayers that include a confession something like this: "and dear God, by the way, would you please forgive me for all the sins I committed today?" If that's the best you can do, then don't bother. Dirty sins are a lot like dirty clothes. They need individual attention.

Confess means "to agree with" or to "say the same thing as." Confession means we say the same about our sin that God says.

God says our sin causes pain, breaks fellowship, lacks love, and drives the nails into Christ's hands and feet.

True confession causes us to deal theologically with personalized Christianity. Confession means we admit our behavior is intricately involved with why Christ had to die. Confession involves entering into the experience of godly sorrow. Paul declared in 2 Corinthians 7:10:

> *"Godly sorrow brings repentance that leads to salvation and leaves no regret, but worldly sorrow brings death." (NIV)*

It breaks my heart when I admit that my selfishness (or whatever) is not only sin, it's part of what drove the nails into the hands and feet of Jesus. During confession, godly sorrow means we replay the scene of our sin and seek to feel what Jesus felt when He watched us do what we did. As we see His breaking heart, we enter into godly sorrow.

Julie has trouble keeping up with her things. I get tired of her constantly calling me to come pick her up at church or the mall or wherever because she has lost her keys again. I remember one Saturday when her passport was in Houston, her cell phone was in Phoenix, and her purse was at the McDonalds in Tucson. No joke.

One Saturday afternoon I pulled into the church parking lot next to Julie's car. I looked in and sure enough there were her keys on the passenger's seat. The car was unlocked for anyone to come by and steal! I was furious. This was the last straw.

I went into the worship center and found Julie at the piano practicing with several ten- and eleven-year-old violinists for a worship performance on Sunday. I was so angry that I walked up the aisle shaking the keys and shouting at Julie, "Do you know where your keys were? Of course not! What am I going to have to do, tie them around your neck?"

I threw the keys down on the piano keyboard and stormed back to my office to work on my sermon on love from 1 Corinthians 13. That is really true. Love was my topic for next Sunday.

I think it's fair to say there was more going on in my life than just Julie's keys. I was obviously angry and struggling with a lot of things. I just dumped it all on Julie. What I did was uncalled for and absolutely wrong.

As I sat in my office thinking about 1 Corinthians 13 and how I had just treated Julie, I began feeling miserably guilty. I decided before I confessed my sin to God, I needed to experience some godly sorrow. So, I closed my eyes and imagined Jesus was watching me do what I just did.

I pictured myself storming down the aisle and yelling at Julie and shaking her keys at her. I imagined Jesus looking at me with such disappointment. I see Him looking at Julie with eyes of hurt and compassion. Julie is seated and I am standing over her, yelling at her. I see the look of terror in Julie's eyes. Jesus is sorry for me, being so out of control. He is sorry for Julie, having to experience my sin. And He is sorry for Himself, because this kind of sin and behavior is what put Him on the cross.

Then, I notice the wide-eyed looks in the faces of the young violinists. They have just witnessed their pastor deliver a vicious scolding to his wife. I see their puzzled looks. I've hurt them, too—any maybe even part of their long-term spiritual journeys.

Now, and only now, am I ready to confess my sin. Confession means we agree with God that what we did was wrong. We resist the temptation to defend our actions or justify our behavior. At this point we are ready to request God's forgiveness. Then we trust God for the cleansing work of grace and forgiveness as promised in 1 John 1:9: "if we confess our sins, he is faithful and just and will forgive us our sins, and purify us from all unrighteousness." (NIV)

By faith we trust that our fellowship with God is restored, and we can once again see and hear Jesus.

Then, and only then, am I in a heartbroken condition that makes me fit to apologize to Julie and to the violinists. My sin was forgiven by both God and Julie, But the hurt I did to my wife lasted for a long time. That is one of the consequences of sin.

Forgotten Sins

Several people in my spiritual growth classes will always ask, "Well, what do I with the sins I can't remember?"

I tell them, "Don't worry about the sins you can't remember"." "Confess the ones you can remember. At the right time and place God will bring to mind any unconfessed sin in your past dirtying up your spirit. When those sins come to mind, take time for godly sorrow, and confess them.

I was out jogging just after dawn on a beautiful morning. The atmosphere was right for a time of worship, praise, and prayer. Suddenly, the Lord brought to my mind a sin I committed in my middle-teenage years. As my inappropriate behavior came to mind, my face began to blush. "This is really strange," I thought. "Here I am out in the middle of the desert, jogging back to the house with nobody around to see me, and I'm blushing." I felt shamed as I considered my past behavior.

I immediately said, "Oh, God, I didn't realize that was down in there." I confessed it before God.

Later, I was in the shower, cleaning up to go to work when I began to review what had just happened. God had so removed the sin from my inner spirit I couldn't even recall what it was. To this day, the sin which caused me to blush remains banished from my conscious memory—so completely did God cleanse it out of my life.

> "Blessed are the pure in heart, for they will see God." Matthew 5:8 (NIV)

Sin unknown for years may not affect our relationship with God. But as soon as the memory surfaces we forfeit fellowship for every moment we allow the sin to remain unprocessed.

Allow me to repeat the two things really important in keeping a clean spirit.

First, "don't self." Always respond positively to the Spirit's promptings. Don't quench the Spirit by choosing self over Spirit.

Second, "don't sin." Sin grieves God, breaks His heart, and devastates our intimate fellowship with the One who is from the beginning.

One more thing is necessary. Since the conscience is the interface between the spirit and the soul, don't ever violate your conscience.

Never Violate Your Conscience

Remember our model of three interlocking concentric circles?

The inside circle is the human spirit where God lives. The middle circle represents the human soul where we live (our mind—intellect, will, and emotions). Finally, the outside circle represents the body.

In examining our model more closely, we might say the intersecting area between soul and body is the five senses. We might say the place where spirit and soul interface is the conscience. Drawing near to God is now a spiritual matter related to how well we follow our consciences. Since we must go through our consciences to enter into God's presence, we must have a clean one.

> *Therefore, brothers and sisters, since we have confidence to enter the Most Holy Place by the blood of Jesus, by a new and living way opened for us through the curtain, that is, his body, and since we have a great priest over the house of God, let us draw near to God with a sincere heart in full assurance of faith, having our hearts sprinkled to cleanse us from a guilty conscience and having our bodies washed with pure water. Let us hold unswervingly to the hope we profess, for he who promised is faithful. Hebrews 10:19-23 (NIV)*

Paul described the conscience as the moral sense God has planted within each of us that tells us God exists. However, the main job of the conscience is to tell us what is right and wrong relative to how it has been trained.

As a result, we need to align our consciences as closely as possible according to biblical truth. We must know the Bible well so our consciences can be accurate in guiding us to identify right from wrong. As we mature, our consciences are much better at determining whether our behavior is right or wrong according to God's principles and His Word.

Several things are involved in developing a biblically trained conscience.

First, we must understand the difference between personal convictions and biblical truth. The pastor of the church I grew up in was instrumental in shaping within me a biblically trained conscience. Of course, like all of us, he was not perfect in his biblical understanding and teaching.

He drilled into our congregation the Baptist denominational teaching that dancing and drinking alcohol were sins. Are either of those injunctions biblical? No. They are Baptist, but not biblical.

Joyous dancing and drinking alcohol are discernable throughout the stories and principles of Scripture. Don't get drunk is what the

Bible teaches. Don't drink at all was his personal conviction—but certainly not a biblical truth.

I have little use for alcohol. My maternal grandfather drank himself to death. One of my aunts did, too. Another aunt and uncle were killed by a drunk driver. My uncle was also driving drunk. Just because I have no use for alcohol does not make drinking alcohol wrong.

The first time I saw two of our church leaders and their wives with cocktails I was scandalized! My respect for them plummeted. I've had to get over that. In that area, I was what Paul called a "weak" Christian.

Second, if your conscience is "weak", strengthen it. Paul uses the term "weak" in Romans 14:1-22 to describe a conscience not aligned with God's truth. Paul used the term "strong" to describe a conscience aligned with biblical truth.

In the first-century church some Christians considered eating meat offered to idols to be unholy and sinful. Others felt they were free in Christ to eat it. Some felt that days like the Sabbath were especially holy and should be treated accordingly. Others felt that no days were special. They were free in Christ to enjoy them all!

Paul agreed with the latter group. He declared in Romans 14:14: "I am convinced, being fully persuaded in the Lord Jesus, that nothing is unclean in itself." (NIV) Again, he wrote in Romans 14:20: "All food is clean." (NIV)

Paul made a plea for unity among both groups in Romans 14:13: "Therefore, let us stop passing judgment on one another." (NIV)

Christians have convictions about all sorts of issues that are not necessarily biblical truth: dancing, drinking alcoholic beverages, smoking, card playing, wearing makeup, Sunday sports, styles of music, hymnals, worship songs, and going to the movies.

When we want to make our personal convictions about any of these areas normative for others, we become ministers of condemnation.

Restricting Our Freedom

Paul lays down several principles about the conscience and how we relate to others.

First, if your conscience is "strong" don't scandalize your "weak" Christian brothers or sisters by exercising your freedom in front of them. Limit your freedom as an act of love:

The strong need not limit their freedom forever. They are to come alongside the weak brothers and sisters and work with them gently to bring them freedom.

Second, if you realize you are weak, then by faith, willpower, prayer, saturating your mind with biblical truth, and spending time with those who are strong, do all you can to find and enjoy your freedom in Christ!

Wherever you are on the spectrum of weak and strong, never violate your conscience. Why? Because a violated conscience impairs our ability to commune with Jesus—Holy Spirit to human spirit. This is why Paul declared in Romans 14:23: "...everything that does not come from faith is sin." (NIV)

A woman once asked me why a group of pastors didn't get together and come up with a list of all the sins so everyone would know what they could or not do. No two pastors could agree on the same list. Second, what is a sin for one person is not necessarily a sin for another, depending on whether the conscience is violated.

Few things are more freeing than a clear conscience. Few things are more inhibiting than a crowded, soiled, guilty conscience. Paul knew that a clean interface between soul and spirit is absolutely critical:

> *"I strive always to keep my conscience clear before God and man." Acts 24:16* (NIV)

The War Within

When I was a young pastor, *Christianity Today* published a practical quarterly journal for pastors called *Leadership Journal*. One article was written by an anonymous pastor detailing his descent into pornography. "An Anatomy of Lust" was a fascinating article. We couldn't pass it around the church office fast enough.

The anonymous pastor was preaching at a revival meeting in a particular city. It was a lovely evening, so he chose to walk back to his hotel. On the way he passed a strip joint. He'd never entered one of these before. He said to himself, "I'll just duck in here and take a quick look." When he got inside, he saw things he had never seen before—never imagined he would see—never planned to see. Unfortunately, he was hooked.

That night in his hotel room, overcome with shame and guilt, he thought, "I'll never see the light of morning. I've committed such a horrible sin that God is going to kill me tonight." He imagined the hotel roof caving in upon him during the night. But, lo and behold, he woke up just as he had every other day of his life.

Pastoral work is hard enough without living a double life. The anonymous pastor detailed the dark side as he struggled with porn. He snuck into peep shows, devoured pornographic magazines, and put dollars in places he shouldn't be putting dollars. The shame and guilt were incredible.

He tried some of the standard ways to find freedom from bondage. "God, take it away!" he cried. But that did not work. He tried willpower with no success. "I will never do it again!" he promised God. But he did. It all proved to be ineffective.

Flying across the western United States, he struggled with how his sin was affecting His marriage. He now had a whole sex life apart from his wife. She knew something was wrong, but couldn't quite put her finger on it. He looked out the window and prayed, "God, since I can't get victory over my sin of pornography, would you just strike me blind? I'm going to close my eyes and while they are closed, I am asking you to strike me blind. He was desperate. However, when he opened his eyes, he could still see the desert out the airplane window. God didn't take away his sight.

He shared this: "The great lie of Playboy magazine and racy movies is that the physical ideal of beauty is attainable and, oh, so close. The truth is that if I sat next to Miss October, she wouldn't give me the time of day."

Sports Illustrated magazine puts out an annual swimsuit issue with increasingly scantily clad women. The first cover photo to cross the line of decency was of supermodel Cheryl Tiegs wearing a fishnet swimsuit.

At this point, the anonymous pastor gained an insight that led to his freedom. He wrote, "I began to realize I can have luscious Cheryl, if I want—teeth flashing, breasts exposed, and coming right at me out of the magazine. I can have luscious Cheryl," he said. "But I can't have Cheryl and also have God."

Two Christian classics, *The City of God* by St. Augustine and *What I Believe* by the 15th century French priest Francois Muriac contained the keys that opened the door to his freedom. The anonymous pastor wrote:

> After brazenly denying the most common reasons I have heard against succumbing to a life filled with lust, Muriac concludes that there is only one reason to seek purity. It is the reason Christ proposed in the Beatitudes: "Blessed are the pure in heart, for they shall see God."
>
> Sins are not a list of petty irritations drawn up for the sake of a jealous God. They are, rather, a description of the impediments to spiritual growth. We are the ones who suffer if we sin, by forfeiting the development of character and Christlikeness that would have resulted if we had not sinned.
>
> Cheryl Tiegs coming toward me out of the page, her teeth flashing, her eyes sparkling, her body glistening, is that City of Man. The pure in heart shall see God. Set against luscious Cheryl, somehow that promise does not seem like much. But that is the lie of the Deceiver. The City of God is the real, the substantial, the whole. What I become as I strengthen my citizenship in that kingdom is far more worthy than anything I could become if all my fantasies were somehow fulfilled.

"I can have my sin if I want to," summarized the anonymous pastor, "but I cannot have my sin and also have pure access to God—and somehow or other, the desire to see God means more than my desire to see Cheryl."

The freedom principles are simple: Don't sin. Don't self. And don't violate your conscience. We can sin if we choose; however, we must remember the degree to which we sin is the degree to which we impair our ability to see and hear from God. *"Blessed are the pure in heart for they shall see God."*

> Dear Jesus,
>
> I pray total cleansing for my dirty heart. Please forgive my sins and enable me to live intimately with you to relationship depths that I never dreamed possible. Help me to grow to spiritual maturity at any price.
>
> Amen.

CHAPTER 14

GOD'S VOICE

One evening I was sitting beside my fiancée in the little church we occasionally attended when we were in college. During the service a woman said to Julie: "I have a prophecy from the Lord for you. You will be like the prophetess, Anna, in Luke 2. You will be widowed after seven years and spend the rest of your life ministering in sweet service to God."

My instinct was to say, "How rude! Why don't you mind your own business." But I held my tongue. Nevertheless, on the evening of our eighth anniversary, I intentionally stayed awake until midnight – just to check that God had not spoken to her. God's voice is not the only voice that speaks.

Self and Satan can both wreak havoc in the lives of Christians who are unable to distinguish among the three.

In Ecclesiastes 5:1-3 Solomon advises us to be wise when we think we hear God's voice and to be careful when we speak to Him.

> "Guard your steps when you go to the house of God. Go near
> to listen rather than to offer the sacrifice of fools, who do not
> know they do wrong. Do not be quick with your mouth; do
> not be hasty in your heart to utter anything before God. God
> is in heaven and you are on earth, so let your words be few.
> A dream comes when there are many cares, and many words
> mark the speech of a fool." (NIV)

Solomon instructs us to draw near and listen. He suggests we stay quiet because God has a better perspective on our lives than we do. We are often so busy instructing God what to do and how to do it that we have trouble hearing His plans. So, be quiet and listen. When He speaks, surrender—and live accordingly.

I was teaching principles of spiritual growth in an old communist factory auditorium to 125 Ukrainian pastors. The daily menu included red borscht, green borscht, and plain borscht depending upon whether the thin soup had red beets, lettuce, or not much at all. An occasional bean was spotted in the bottom of some bowls.

The pastors were hungry for Bible teaching. In contrast to pastoral seminars in America, these men found seats early. No one stood in the hallway talking during the sessions. They were afraid they might miss something.

The distractions were few—no television, no movies, no shopping, no ball games, no concerts—so to maximize our time, several of the pastors and I gathered after dinner each night for impromptu discussions.

One night an elderly gentleman was visibly agitated that a young, inexperienced American like me would presume to teach him and his cohorts about the Bible. His speech was electrifying: "We've had more experiences with God and suffering than he will ever know!" He shouted, "We've been tested by fire. What does he know that we don't know? Why should we listen to him?"

Some were embarrassed by his outburst. Some agreed. Every eye was on me. I turned to the white-haired Ukrainian pastor who had suffered so much during 70 years of communist persecution, and said,

"Do you realize how humbling it is for me to presume to teach you anything. I've walked through your cemeteries and seen thousands of tree-stump-shaped tombstones—symbolizing so many lives cut off before their time. I know Stalin sold your grain to Germany that year to raise cash and five million Ukrainians starved. I've seen the thousands of grave markers dated 1941-42 when the German invasion and harsh winter killed millions more. Twenty years ago, I read *The Gulag Archipelago* and *One Day in the Life of Ivan Denisovich,* by Alexander Solzhenitsyn, and God put it in my heart to pray for you."

When I mentioned those books chronicling the prison experience and suffering under communist rule, the charged atmosphere dissipated. I slowly proceeded, "I am overwhelmed that—after years of praying for your strength, protection, safety, and courage—I am here as your teacher. May I sit quietly at your feet and learn from you for a while? Please tell me your stories."

So, they did. They told of torture and scars. They told of the sufferings. It broke my heart as I listened to a young lieutenant air force pilot tell of a recent confrontation with soldiers in his squadron who demanded either his renunciation of Christ or his death by their hands. They expected him to meet them in an abandoned building on base at noon the next day. He went expecting to be beaten to death. They never came. They were testing his commitment to Christ. They never bothered him again.

These Ukrainians had experienced the fellowship of sharing in Christ's sufferings. They knew the cost of following Jesus. I decided to begin the next morning session with a question about what it might cost to hear God speak.

"How many of you want to hear God speak?" Every hand raised high. I was not surprised. Every Christian wants to hear God speak.

I asked them a second question: "Have you ever wondered why there are so few prophets in the Bible?" I paused to let that sink in and then paraphrased several Bible scenarios.

Take Off Your Clothes

God said to Hosea, "Do you want to hear me speak?"

"I'd love to be your prophet and hear you speak."

"Then, go marry a prostitute."

One day God asked Jeremiah, "Do you want to hear me speak? Do you want to be my prophet?"

"God, I'm too young to be a prophet; but I'd love to hear you speak."

So, God spoke to Jeremiah, "You will be my prophet. However, the price of hearing my voice is high. The people will curse you, mock you, toss you in jail, and bind you in chains. They will throw you in cisterns and beat you senseless. They will humiliate you and position you in stocks in the marketplaces." Worst of all, we know now that the people never believed a single word he said.

One day God commanded Isaiah, "Take off your clothes."

"Why?"

"Don't ask me why. Just take them off."

"Well, for how long?"

"Until I tell you to put them on again."

Isaiah stripped off his clothes. Imagine the scene as He walked naked down the streets of Jerusalem. "Hey, Isaiah," mocked the people, "where are your clothes?"

"I took them off."

"Why?"

"Well, God told me to."

Can you imagine the looks Isaiah got when said, "Well, I heard this little voice ..."

After three years, God spoke, "Isaiah, put on your clothes and declare this word from Me: 'As I have bared your buttocks, so I will bare the buttocks of Egypt and let the Assyrians spank them.'" For three years, Isaiah walked around bare-bottomed, and the message wasn't even for Israel!

I paused in my teaching and looked into the faces of these precious Ukrainian men and women who knew how to suffer for Christ. I asked again: "Now, how many of you want to hear God speak?" Not a hand went up. I waited quietly. They knew the cost like few others. Then, one hand raised uncertainly . . . and then another . . . and then every hand . . . some raised both hands.

"Then," I said, "let's proceed."

In Exodus 20:18-19 the Israelites refused God's invitation to come to the mountain and hear Him speak:

> *"When the people saw the thunder and lightning and heard the trumpet and saw the mountain in smoke, they trembled with fear. They stayed at a distance and said to Moses, 'Speak to us yourself and we will listen. But do not have God speak to us or we will die.'" (NIV)*

When we personally hear God speaking, life will never the same!

In a day when the secular world is crying for answers, too many Christians are stuttering. They have no word from the Lord. Some don't listen because they are afraid of what he might say. Others don't listen because they are just plain lazy!

This is a paradox. While hearing from God might cost us our lives, the voice of God opens the floodgates so the living water of the Holy Spirit might flow into our innermost beings (John 7:37-39). While hearing from God might cost us our lives, following the voice of God leads to abundant life (John 10:10).

We must be careful when we think God is the one speaking to us. We can be fooled. As we mentioned earlier, God, Satan, and Self all have a stake in this business.

Many of us have been burned by people who say things like "God told me" or "I have a word from the Lord for you."

I'm always leery about people who tell me God has given them a message for me. My first thought is, "Why didn't God just give the message to me?"

Without pausing, one woman launched into a detailed pronouncement that my wife Julie and I would soon suffer a divorce. I had neglected my wife, she said, and failed to build the kind of marriage God intended for pastors. Thus, the penalty would be the forfeiture of my marriage.

I knew enough not to laugh out loud or tell her what she could do with her message. Just for fun, I decided to play this out. After all, the pages of scripture are filled with stories of unusual people who did strange things as God led them to pronounce, "The Lord says...!"

I called one of my spiritual advisers. "Jack," I said, "I need your advice. I'm 99 percent sure her message was not from God. Just help me verify for certain."

He responded, "Did the warning give any hope for reconciling the marriage and avoiding the divorce?"

"No."

"When God warned of doom in the Bible, He usually provided a means for avoiding the consequences—often by repentance and restitution. Did the message provide any hope for averting the divorce?"

"No."

"Then the message was not from God."

"Thanks."

The reason we struggle at times to listen to God is because our spirit is still immature. We are not really sure how to hear Him speak.

The seminary I attended required approximately thirty different classes for a Master of Divinity degree. Of those thirty different classes, not one dealt with the spiritual dimensions of hearing God speak. Looking back now, I see my seminary experience was focused on becoming biblically smart and pastorally efficient. Cultivating the spiritual life was an afterthought!

Elijah organized a school for young, aspiring prophets. Today, some Roman Catholic teachers say, "Do it like this." Some Pentecostals say, "No, you do it like this." Some evangelicals say, "This is how you do it." Some Dispensationalists say, "God does not do it." I think younger Christians are so confused they don't even try to listen.

Another reason we are reticent to hear God speak is because we are afraid of losing credibility if we announce what we think God told us, only to discover later that we were wrong.

Occasionally older Christians tell me God promised them they would live to see the glorious return of Christ at the rapture. They are certain the rapture of the church will come during their lifetime. I have buried most of those folks. They mistook the voice of self for the voice of God.

We were considering relocating our church operations. Full parking lots and six weekend worship services impaired our ability to reach more people for Christ. Standing in front of the bathroom mirror one Saturday, I almost dropped my razor at the thought that flashed into my mind. Instead of going to all the trouble and expense of relocating, why not purchase the eight houses surrounding our property? We could build a new worship center and expand our parking lots to make room for new growth. I thanked God for revealing this new course of action.

I told our church leaders what God told me and led the church to make plans to purchase the adjoining houses. The deed restrictions of the surrounding subdivision required that every one of the 100 homeowners approve the required rezoning and sale. The homeowners were not pleased; nevertheless, we forged ahead. Six months, numerous unpleasant neighborhood association meetings and well over 100 irate neighbors later, we called off the deal.

I was licking my wounds when a wise saint said to me, "You ignored the Tenth Commandment: 'You shall not covet your neighbor's house.'"

I'm not certain whether it was the voice of self or of Satan I heard that Saturday morning while I was shaving. I do know this, the voice I thought certainly came from God was not the voice of God.

God speaks in a variety of ways. The following list, in no particular order, details some of those ways:

The Bible:

> *Your word is a lamp for my feet and a light on my path. Psalm 119:105 (NIV)*

Jesus Christ:

> *In the past God spoke to our ancestors through the prophets at many times and in various ways, but in these last days he has spoken to us by his Son, whom he appointed heir of all things, and through whom he made the universe. The Son is the radiance of God's glory and the exact representation of his being, sustaining all things by his powerful word. Hebrews 1:1-3 (NIV)*

Signs and wonders:

> *Then Peter said, "Silver or gold I do not have, but what I do have I give you. In the name of Jesus Christ of Nazareth, walk." Acts 3:6 (NIV)*

Tests:

> *Gideon said to God, "If you will save Israel by my hand as you have promised—look, I will place a wool fleece on the threshing floor. If there is dew only on the fleece and all the ground is dry, then I will know that you will save Israel by my hand, as you said." And that is what happened. Judges 6:36-38 (NIV)*

Godly People:

> *Now then, my children, listen to me [Wisdom];*
> *blessed are those who keep my ways.*

Listen to my instruction and be wise;
do not disregard it.
Blessed are those who listen to me. Proverbs 8:32-34 (NIV)

Children At Bedtime:

A third time the LORD called Samuel. And Samuel got up
and went to Eli and said, "Here I am; you called me." Then
Eli realized that the LORD was calling the boy. 9 So Eli told
Samuel, "Go and lie down, and if he calls you, say, 'Speak,
LORD, for your servant is listening.'" So Samuel went and lay
down in his place. 1 Samuel 3:8-9 (NIV)

The Creation:

For since the creation of the world God's invisible qualities—
his eternal power and divine nature—have been clearly seen,
being understood from what has been made, so that people
are without excuse. Romans 1:20 (NIV)

Preachers and Prophets:

During this time some prophets came down from Jerusalem to
Antioch. One of them, named Agabus, stood up and through
the Spirit predicted that a severe famine would spread over
the entire Roman world. (This happened during the reign of
Claudius.) Acts 11:27-28 (NIV)

Donkeys:

The donkey said to Balaam, "Am I not your own donkey, which
you have always ridden, to this day?" Numbers 22:30 (NIV)

Bushes:

There the angel of the LORD appeared to him in flames of
fire from within a bush. Moses saw that though the bush was
on fire it did not burn up. ... When the LORD saw that he had
gone over to look, God called to him from within the bush,
"Moses! Moses!" And Moses said, "Here I am." Exodus 3:2 and
4 (NIV)

Angels:

In the sixth month of Elizabeth's pregnancy, God sent the angel Gabriel to Nazareth, a town in Galilee, to a virgin pledged to be married to a man named Joseph, a descendant of David. The virgin's name was Mary. The angel went to her and said, "Greetings, you who are highly favored! The Lord is with you." Luke 1:26-28 (NIV)

The Angel of the Lord:

Then he reached out his hand and took the knife to slay his son. But the angel of the LORD called out to him from heaven, "Abraham! Abraham!" "Here I am," he replied. Genesis 22:10-11 (NIV)

God's Glory:

Then Moses said, "Now show me your glory." And the LORD said, "I will cause all my goodness to pass in front of you, and I will proclaim my name, the LORD, in your presence." Exodus 33:18-19 (NIV)

Circumstances:

Paul and his companions traveled throughout the region of Phrygia and Galatia, having been kept by the Holy Spirit from preaching the word in the province of Asia. When they came to the border of Mysia, they tried to enter Bithynia, but the Spirit of Jesus would not allow them to. So they passed by Mysia and went down to Troas. Acts 16:6-8 (NIV)

Reasoning:

Come now, let us reason together, says the LORD. Isaiah 1:18 (RSV)

Dreams and visions:

And afterward,
*   I will pour out my Spirit on all people.*
Your sons and daughters will prophesy,

> *your old men will dream dreams,*
>
> *your young men will see visions. Joel 2:28 (NIV)*

Failures:

> *Then Peter remembered the word Jesus had spoken: "Before the rooster crows, you will disown me three times." And he went outside and wept bitterly. Matthew 26:75 (NIV)*

THE human spirit:

> *Then you will call on me and come and pray to me, and I will listen to you. You will seek me and find me when you seek me with all your heart. Jeremiah 29:12-13 (NIV)*

God speaks in many ways. As we mature into spiritual mothers and fathers, we become increasingly sensitive to the voice of God in our human spirit. When properly cultivated the human spirit can be quite useful in hearing God speak. In his book *Faith Tried and Triumphant*, D. Martyn Lloyd-Jones wrote about the almost mystical approach for hearing God speak Holy Spirit to human spirit.

Then God sometimes answers directly in our spirit. The prophet said, "I will watch and see what he will say in me." Habakkuk 2:1 (JUB)

God speaks to me by speaking in me. He can so lay something upon the mind that we are certain of the answer. He can impress something upon our spirits in an unmistakable manner. We find ourselves unable to get away from an impression that is on our mind or heart. We try to rid ourselves of it, but back it comes. So does God answer at times.[44]

Whenever I sense what may be a word from God, I refuse to accept it until I carefully consider whether I am hearing from God, myself, or Satan. My overriding principle is in dividing between soul and spirit is Hebrews 4:12:

> *"For the word of God is alive and active. Sharper than any double-edged sword, it penetrates even to dividing soul and spirit, joints and marrow; it judges the thoughts and attitudes of the heart." (NIV)*

I try not to do anything until I am certain who is speaking. Only then will I act upon what I hear. When people say, "God told me..."

I often respond, "How did you know the words were from God?" If they can't give a definitive answer I advise, "Then, don't do anything until you know who is speaking. You don't want to make a mistake and follow the wrong voice."

Over the years, I have developed a biblical checklist of what I think God's voice sounds like. The list is in broad generalizations and is certainly not complete, nor foolproof. No one point is sufficient to prove or disprove the voice of God. Nevertheless, I believe these principles are helpful when they line up in a sensible, godly fashion.

1. I never act solely based on what I think I hear in my inner spirit. I seek counsel from trusted advisers who help me verify whether I am on the right track. There is wisdom in many counselors. (Proverb 11:14).

"Every matter may be established by the testimony of two or three witnesses" taught both Moses and Jesus with good reason. (See Deuteronomy 19:15; Matthew 18:16.) These verses remind me never to strike out in announcement or in action without first testing what I think God said with trusted spiritual advisors.

2. God speaks in my innermost spirit; self or Satan speaks in my soul.

Notice again the three parts of man: spirit, soul, and body. The Word of God obviously refers to the Bible as well as to the Lord Jesus Christ whom John identifies in chapter one of his gospel as the "Word of God." The Word of God is a sharp scalpel slicing between soul and spirit in order to help us discern whether the voice we hear emanates from our spirit or soul.

The Bible in conjunction with the promptings of Jesus are basic tools for hearing God speak.

Many wonder whether Satan can inhabit the minds of Christians. Let me make it simple. Who among us has not sensed in our thoughts the temptations of Satan?

Let me give you an example of someone allowing Satan to take control of their mind. On the way to the cross:

> *"Jesus began to explain to His disciples that he must go to Jerusalem and ... be killed and on the third day be raised to life."*

"Peter took him aside and began to rebuke him. "Never Lord!" he said, "This shall never happen to you!"

Jesus turned and said to Peter, "Get behind me, Satan! You are a stumbling block to me; you do not have in mind the concerns of God, but merely human concerns." Matthew 16:21-23 (NIV)

You've had a really bad day when Jesus calls you Satan!

Peter lost control of his soul (mind) to Satan. God will never take control of our souls. He wants our souls free to make our own choices regarding his will. Satan, on the other hand, will do everything possible to control our minds.

Our inner spirits are safe and secure from Satanic attack because God alone has access to our inner human spirit.

Following the guidelines of Hebrews 4:12, I quiet down my mind and allow the Word of God to "divide between soul and spirit." As I listen for God to speak, I try to discern whether what I hear emanates from my soul (my mind) or from my deep, inner, human spirit. Discerning between "soul and spirit" requires patience, practice, and careful cultivation.

3. God tends to speak with gentle leadings in contrast to what I often perceive to be the compulsive, clamoring, loud demands of self or Satan.

Remember how God spoke to Elijah? He was not in the whirlwind, the earthquake, nor the fire. When all got quiet, He spoke with a still, small voice (see 1 Kings 19:11-13).

I remember being pressured by a pushy used car salesman to buy a particular car. He told me things like, "You'd better hurry up. I have another couple who want this car! They are trying to arrange financing right now. They will return at any minute. If you want this car, you need to make an offer quickly." I do not like that kind of pressure—especially on big decisions like buying a car. I turned my back and walked away.

Listening for the real voice of God is not at all like that. The Word of God is open to reason. He seldom urges sudden action without giving us time to think through the issues. I must differentiate between the promptings of God and my drivenness to fulfill my own hurried and harried agenda.

4. God's voice produces freedom. Self's or Satan's voice produces bondage.

> In Matthew 11:30, Jesus says, *"My yoke is easy and my burden is light." (NIV)*

I was sitting high up on Skyline Drive overlooking the city of Tucson one evening when I felt an overwhelming burden to reach the entire city for Christ. If I am not careful, I can become frustratingly overburdened by biting off more ministry than God intends for me to chew. God was not calling me to reach the entire city of Tucson. God has called many pastors to share in the work.

5. God tends to speak when I am consciously seeking Him. Self or Satan tends to speak with sudden intrusions of thoughts into the mind.

Jeremiah reported God as saying:

> *"Then you will call on me and come and pray to me, and I will listen to you. You will seek me and find me when you seek me with all your heart." Jeremiah 29:12-13 (NIV)*

During the first three months I was pastor, the church filled quickly to capacity. People were standing outside the doors listening to big outdoor speakers. No more seats were available inside.

One Sunday morning, on the spur of the moment, I announced that God had just told me how to fix our overcrowded seating problems. He wanted us to remodel our fellowship hall into worship space. At the close of the service one of our deacons quietly handed me a tape measure from the back of his truck.

"Here, I'll lend you this for a week. Why don't you measure and see if God is the one behind your proposal." He winked as he left.

So, I measured and discovered that our fellowship hall was two feet wider and four feet longer than our chapel—hardly enough room to make remodeling worthwhile. The next Sunday, I walked to the pulpit and informed the people that God had changed His mind. Everybody had a good laugh, and I learned a lesson. Both self and Satan may inject thoughts and impressions into my mind when I'm not seeking God. God's voice is most often heard when I am diligently listening for it.

6. When God speaks there is a definite sense that everything is under control. When self or Satan speaks there is an inner sense that something is out of control.

Occasionally, I counsel people who are in the throes of life-changing decisions. They have evaluated the pros and cons, prayed earnestly, often fasted, and still have no clear word from God. As they struggle, nothing makes sense, and everything seems out of control.

One bit of advice I give is never to proceed until all things are done "decently and in order." 1 Corinthians 14:40 (RSV) If there is any feeling that something is amiss or not properly ordered, then postpone the decision until things begin to clear up. When we finally hear from God, the path will be orderly and make perfect sense.

Many decisions have deadlines. We seldom have unlimited time to make a choice. At decision time, if we have not yet made a choice, I encourage godly Christians to do whatever they feel like doing and trust that God has put the right feelings and emotions into your hearts. I can give this advice because David declared:

> *"Take delight in the Lord and He will give you the desires of your heart." Psalm 7:4 (NIV)*

This does not mean that if we delight in God that He will give us whatever we ask for. It means that if we are seeking first the Kingdom and thus delighting in God, He will put the right desires in our hearts.

By the way, I never share this verse with people whose lives give little evidence of seeking first the Kingdom or of delighting in Him.

7. God gives clear-cut, specific directions. Self or Satan often communicate in confused, uncertain wonderings.

Julie and I often pray for God to make things so clear that we can't miss them.

I've had heart arrhythmias for much of my life. Pacemakers can speed up a slow or faltering heart. But my problem was a "runaway heart." In seconds, my heart could go to over 225 beats per minute. The next thing I knew, I was on the floor until the rapid beats subsided and I could get up.

Medicines worked to keep my heart under control as we struggled with the decision to get an artificial electrical implant—or not. The only way to control a runaway heart is to burn away the normal electrical circuits. This procedure is not reversible. It is a decision that would disable my heart forever.

As we prayed and listened for God, we sensed Him saying to be patient. He would soon make the decision so clear we couldn't miss it. Suddenly, the medicines failed. I could not walk up the stairs without my heart running away in potentially fatal rhythms. There were no more decisions to make. I got the device immediately.

8. God convicts of specific sins. Self or Satan often accuses in broad generalities that leave a lingering sense of haunting and unfocused guilt.

In John 16:8 Jesus said that the Holy Spirit *"will convict the world of sin, righteousness, and judgment."* (HCSB) My experience is that when the Holy Spirit convicts of sin, He is quite specific: "At 4:00 p.m. today you used abusive and hurtful words as you raised your voice to Julie because she lost her keys again."

I know exactly what I did and when I did it. I can now confess my sin and receive spiritual cleansing and not worry or ruminate about my sin anymore.

Self or Satan, on the other hand, often leave an unfocused sense of haunting guilt.

When I feel accused or have a nagging sense of unspecified guilt, I pause and consider why I feel so guilty. If there is no conviction over a specific sin, I know that the feelings emanate from the "accuser of our brothers and sisters." Revelation 12:10 (NIV) Or it comes from other internal, personal issues that need attention. I deal accordingly by using spiritual warfare to overcome Satan or by getting control of my thought life.

9. God speaks with 100% truth that can be tested by the Word of God. Self or Satan often traffic in lies, deceit, and half-truths.

One justification of unbiblical behavior that I often hear is from Christians who are planning to marry non-Christians. They tell me that after much prayer they have heard God tell them it's okay for them to proceed with the marriage.

However, the Bible is clear that Christians are never to marry non-Christians. Many ignore those instructions and get married anyway. The word of God divides the truth between spirit and soul. They chose the soul route. Many are divorced less than five years later.

Filtering my thoughts for truth and error is a constant exercise. There's a good reason to know that Satan is "the accuser of our brothers and sisters!"

I find it easy to lie to myself. I can preach what I consider to be a poor sermon and berate myself with thoughts like, "I am the worst preacher who ever preached." Is that true? No. The truth is, maybe last Sunday was not my best, but, thankfully, the Holy Spirit can make something out of nothing.

I can come home after a demoralizing elders' meeting and feel isolated and alone. "Nobody loves me," I think. Is that true? No. This is not God speaking. This is my self, lying to myself. Julie loves me. My mommy loves me. God loves me. There are a lot of people who love me!

I can forget being at the hospital to pray for a church member's surgery. The family is not pleased. Soon, I am telling myself, "I can't do anything right. I am a failure as a pastor."

Is that true? No. I do lots of things right. I want no lies or half-truths in my mind. Life is hard enough to handle with the truth; it is impossible to navigate successfully when the mind is filled with lies and deceit.

10. God's voice always leads to a deep, abiding sense of peace. Self or Satan do not.

> *"Do not be anxious about anything, but in every situation, by prayer and petition, with thanksgiving, present your requests to God. And the peace of God, which transcends all understanding, will guard your hearts and your minds in Christ Jesus." Philippians 4:6-7 (NIV)*

When God speaks, I have a deep sense of peace that lets me know that I am within the boundaries of God's will. When I step out of bounds playing basketball, the referee's whistle stops play until he/she can sort out what happened.

I consider the peace of God to be like a referee with his whistle. When I am not hearing God clearly, I often step out of bounds. The Holy Spirit blows His whistle to stop the game. The ball is put back into play and the game goes on. As long as I stay within the lines the game proceeds smoothly.

When I'm inside the lines I have a deep sense of peace that all is well.

I often meditate by entering into the spirit of Psalm 131. If I can't find this peace, I am likely on the wrong track:

> *My heart is not proud, O Lord, my eyes are not haughty;*
> *I do not concern myself with great matters or things too*
> *wonderful for me. But I have calmed and quieted myself, I am*
> *like a weaned child with its mother; like a weaned child I am*
> *content. Psalm 131:1-2 (NIV)*

I want to hear God speak. I want to recognize God's voice and not be deceived by Satan's voice or mine. Undoubtedly, we will all make mistakes in "dividing soul and spirit" and in recognizing God's voice.

However, the only thing worse than making mistakes is not listening in the first place.

> *Dear Father,*
>
> *Speak clearly to me so that I might know your will whenever*
> *necessary. Enable me to discern who is speaking in any*
> *situation. Guide me in dividing soul from spirit as you mature*
> *me to become a spiritual mother or father any price.*
>
> *Amen.*

CHAPTER 15

WHY BOTHER TO GROW SPIRITUALLY?

Whether or not we grow up makes a difference. Consider the hypothetical lives of two men, Sam and Gary. Actually, this story is not hypothetical. It happens all the time.

On the graph below, the horizontal axis represents increasing age. The vertical axis represents Christlikeness.

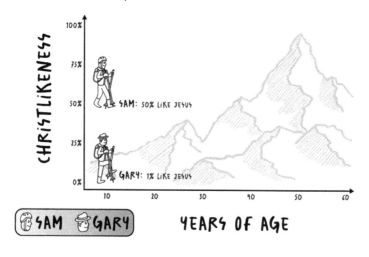

The *Christlikeness scale* is exaggerated for emphasis. No one is 100 percent, or fifty percent, or even ten percent like Jesus. Compared to Him, our Christlikeness is negative infinity. We are not at all like Jesus. The best Christlikeness we can hope for will hardly register on the vertical scale. However, the graphs are skewed to make a point.

Imagine that Sam grew up in a solid Christian home, attended Sunday School, memorized Bible verses, and sang the praises of God from his earliest childhood years. One Sunday morning, this ten-year-old surrendered his life to Christ. On that day we might have said: "He is such a good little boy. He is so well behaved and nice. He's well on his way to Christlikeness—maybe 'fifty percent' like Jesus."

On the same Sunday, ten-year-old Gary boarded a church bus in the slums of the city and rode to church for the first time in his life. His family upbringing was dysfunctional. He never knew his dad. He was in trouble with the law at an early age. In Sunday School that morning, Gary pulled the girls' pigtails and splashed paint on a teacher's dress. One of the teachers said, "Let's send the bus down a different street next week. He's not at all like Jesus!"

However, during the Bible story time, Gary sat transfixed as he heard about the love of Jesus. During a moment of invitation, Gary decided that he, too, wanted to surrender his life to Christ. He maybe started his Christian life "ten percent" like Jesus. Of course, Gary did not begin there, but we've got to start someplace. Remember, I have skewed the numbers to make a point.

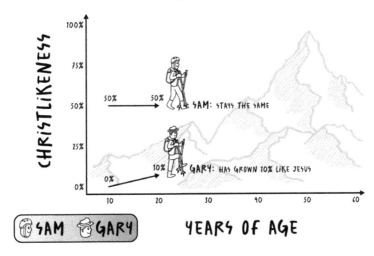

During his college years, Sam studied hard and dated the right women—just as we might expect of a young man with his background and values. He went to church every Sunday. When he earned money, he tithed right off the top, ten percent. He was simply acting out the same values he was taught as a child.

Many commented, "What a great young man. He is every bit as sweet and kind as when he was a child. He still appears to be about 'fifty percent' like Christ." Notice, he's not growing spiritually. He's just doing the things that he needs to grow consistently the same rate that he grew in his childhood.

On the other hand, by the age of twenty, Gary was more likely to shoplift than to get a job. He dated women with rather poor values and morals. He struggled; but he was trying to get his life together and even grow in Christ. He attended church occasionally. He's doing his best to be the spiritual man he's been encouraged to become. As we examine his spiritual progress, we might say that at the age of twenty, Gary had matured to perhaps "twenty percent" like Christ.

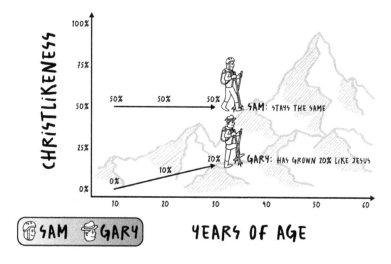

By the age of thirty, Sam was a deacon in his church. He occasionally shared his faith. He attended church regularly. He tithed as he had done since childhood. He married the right girl and had several adorable children. People often said, "He is as good a Christian as he ever was!"

By age thirty, Gary's marriage failed. He bounced around from job to job. However, he was finding new solace and strength in God. He went to church almost every Sunday. He was a long way from being like Christ, but he had grown significantly as a Christian. He now looked "thirty percent" like Jesus.

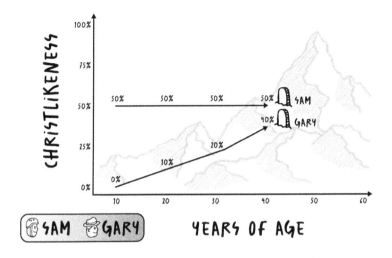

At forty, Sam was a well-respected leader in his church. He was chairman of the elder body. He taught witnessing classes. He and his family tithed regularly. Still "fifty percent!"

Gary continued his slow-but-steady growth in Christ. By forty, most of his personal difficulties were resolved. Spiritually speaking, he still had a long way to go. He was fairly regular in church attendance. He read his Bible occasionally and even gave some money when he went to church. We might say that he matured to be "forty percent" like Jesus.

Tragically, at the age of forty, both Sam and Gary died on the same day in separate car accidents. At Sam's funeral, the pastor said, "We're certainly going to miss Sam. He was one of our finest men. He leaves behind a loving family and a reputation as a man of integrity. He supported the church. He tithed and witnessed and cared for those in need. We will remember him as a fine, upstanding Christian man who was just as good and wholesome as an adult as he was as a child." He finished his time on earth at "fifty percent" like Jesus.

That afternoon at Gary's funeral, the pastor did not have as many good things to say. To all outward appearances, Gary was not quite as good a Christian as Sam. Sam was "fifty percent" like Jesus, while Gary was only "forty percent" like Jesus.

But whoever said that life ends at death?

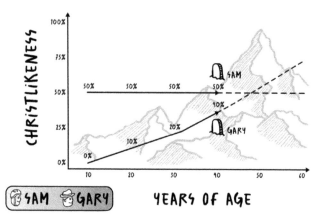

The importance of spiritual growth is demonstrated dramatically when we extend both lines out into eternity. The horizontal tracking is consistent with who Sam is—great start, didn't grow spiritually. Basically, he rested on his laurels and continued to look about "fifty percent" like Jesus throughout his lifetime.

When we extrapolate Gary's line out into eternity, it continues to slope upward at the same rate. This upward line is consistent with who he became as a result of his spiritual growth. Off into eternity, Gary quickly surpasses Sam.

> Jesus declared, *"From everyone who has been given much, much will be demanded; and from the one who has been entrusted with much, much more will be asked"* (Luke 12:48).
>
> Gary didn't start with much; but, look what he did with it! Jesus continued, *"Well done, good and faithful servant! You have been faithful with a few things (on earth); I will put you in charge of many things (in Heaven). Come and share your master's happiness!"* (Matthew 25:21).

It is vital that we mature at any price. We are not living the Christian life for forty, fifty, or even seventy years. We're in this for eternity.

> *Dear Father,*
>
> *Please take me far along the journey into the mountain peaks of resurrection life with Jesus. I want to be a spiritual mother/father at any price.*
>
> *Amen*

ENDNOTES

[1] Miles Stanford, *Principles of Spiritual Growth*, (Lincoln, Nebraska:Back to the Bible, 1968).

[2] Watchman Nee, *The Release of the Spirit,* (Sure Foundation, 1965).

[3] Watchman Nee, *The Spiritual Man in Three Volumes*, (New York:Christian Fellowship Publishers, 1968).

[4] Hannah Hurnard, *Hind's Feet On High Places*, (London:Olive Press, 1972).

[5] John Bunyan, *Pilgrims Progress*, ed. W. R. Owens (Oxford:Oxford World's Classics Edition, 2003).

[6] Hannah Hurnard, *Mountains Of Spices*, (Wheaton:Tyndale House, 1983).

[7] Jeanne Guyon, *Experiencing the Depths of Jesus Christ* (Jacksonville, FL:SeedSowers, 1975).

[8] David Ferguson and Theresa Ferguson, *Intimate Encounters*(Austin, Texas: Intimacy Press, 1997).

[9] David Ferguson, *Relation Foundations* (Austin, Texas:Relationship Press, 2004).

[10] Charles Spurgeon, *Lectures to My Students*. (Grand Rapids:Zondervan, 1996).

[12] Miles Stanford, *Principles of Spiritual Growth*, (Lincoln, Nebraska:Back to the Bible, 1968), pp. 30-31.

[13] Raymond McHenry, *McHenry's Stories for the Soul* (Peabody, Massachusetts:Hendrickson Publishers, 2001), pp. 46-47.

[14] Story told in the sermon, *The Cost of Discipleship*, by Dickson Rial, Garland, Texas, October, 1966.

[15] Steve May, *The Story File*, (Peabody, Massachusetts:Hendrickson Publishers, 2000), p.127.

[16] J.M. Barrie, *Peter and Wendy*, (London: Hodder & Stoughton,1911).

[17] Mark Bubeck, *The Adversary*, (Chicago:Moody Press, 1975).

[18] Tommy Armour;, *How to Play Your Best Golf All of the Time,* (New York:Simon and Schuster, 1953).

[19] Hannah Hurnard, *Hind's Feet On High Places*, (London:Olive Press, 1972) XX.

[20] Hannah Hurnard, *Mountains Of Spices*, (Wheaton:Tyndale House, 1983).

[21] "The Letter of Lentulus" is an apocryphal letter written by Publius Lentulus who was said to be Governor of Judea before Pontius Pilate. The letter purportedly was written to the Roman Senate to give a physical description of Jesus. The letter was most likely written in the 2nd century A.D.

[22] Miles Stanford, *Principles of Spiritual Growth*, (Lincoln, Nebraska:Back to the Bible, 1968), p 25.

[23] C. S. Lewis, *Out Of The Silent Planet,* (New York:Simon & Schuster, 2003).

[24] C. S. Lewis, *Perelandra,* (New York:Simon & Schuster, 2003).

[25] C. S. Lewis, *That Hideous Strength*, (New York:Simon & Schuster, 2003).

[26] Dietrich Bonhoeffer, *The Cost of Discipleship*, (New York:Macmillan 1966).

[27] *The Bridges of Madison County* is a 1995 American film based on the best-selling novel of the same name by Robert James Waller.

[28] Miles Stanford, *Principles of Spiritual Growth*, (Lincoln, Nebraska:Back to the Bible, 1968), pp. 25-26.

[29] Dietrich Bonhoeffer, *The Cost of Discipleship,,;* (New York:Macmillan; New York, New York; 1966).

[30] Dale Martin Stone, "Sourcebook of Poetry" quoted in *The Tale of the Tardy Oxcart* by Chuck Swindoll, W Publishing Group; Nashville, Tennessee; 1998.

[31] Miles Stanford, *Principles of Spiritual Growth*, (Lincoln, Nebraska:Back to the Bible, 1968), p.14.

[32] Miles Stanford, *Principles of Spiritual Growth*, (Lincoln, Nebraska:Back to the Bible, 1968). p.11.

[33] A. W. Tozer, *The Best of A. W. Tozer*, ed. Warren Wiersbe, (Grand Rapids:Baker Book House, 1978), pp.103-105.

[34] Miles Stanford, *Principles of Spiritual Growth*, (Lincoln, Nebraska:Back to the Bible, 1968), p.12.

[35] Miles Stanford, *Principles of Spiritual Growth*, (Lincoln, Nebraska:Back to the Bible, 1968), pp. 30-31.

[36] David Ferguson and Theresa Ferguson, *Intimate Encounters,* (Austin, Texas:Intimacy Press, 1997), pp.1-16.

[37] George Barna, *Thinking Like Jesus: Make the Right Decision Every Time*, (Ventura, California:Issachar Resources, 2003), p.2.

[38] George Barna, *Thinking Like Jesus: Make the Right Decision Every Time*, (Ventura, California:Issachar Resources, 2003), pp.47-55.

[39] 3. Watchman Nee, *The Spiritual Man in Three Volumes*, (New York:Christian Fellowship Publishers, 1968).

[40] R. Kent Hughes, *1001 Great Stories and Quotes*, (Wheaton:Tyndale House, 1998), p.62

[41] Elton Gilliam, *29:50 Plan*.

[42] MacCartney's Illustrations, consolidated.

[43] Jeanne Guyon, *Experiencing the Depths of Jesus Christ*, (Jacksonville, Florida:Seed Sowers, 1975).

[44] D. Martin Lloyd-Jones, , *Faith Tried and Triumphant*, (Grand Rapids:Baker Books, 1994), p.30.

[45] David Ferguson, *Relation Foundations*, (Austin, Texas:Relationship Press, 2004), pp.47-58.

[46] Ibid; pp.42-46.

[47] Ibid; pp.59-63.

[48] Tony Campolo, *Let Me Tell You a Story*, (Nashville:Thomas Nelson, 2000), pp.85-86.

Printed in the USA
CPSIA information can be obtained
at www.ICGtesting.com
LVHW011911160324
774636LV00010B/337